AF226548

The Stress-Free Money Blueprint

A Financial Literacy Guide to Budgeting Paychecks, Escaping Debt, Investing Early, Building Wealth, and Buying Your First Home

Patty R. Adams

Cantelune Press

2026

Contents

Thank You for Reading!

I hope you found The Stress-Free Money Blueprint helpful and enjoyable!

Your feedback is invaluable to me and helps others discover this book.

If you could take a moment to leave a review,

I'd greatly appreciate it!

Patty

Visit the Cantelune Press website for more compassionate books that meet you where you are! https://cantelunepress.com/

Introduction

You're scrolling through social media, watching friends post about their dream vacations, new apartments, and seemingly perfect lives, while you're sitting there wondering how you'll make rent *and* pay off your credit card this month.

Sound familiar? You're not alone. In 2026, nearly 73% of young adults report feeling anxious about their financial future, and the majority admit they have no clear plan for building wealth or achieving financial independence.

I wrote this book because I'm tired of seeing talented, ambitious people held back by financial confusion and fear. You deserve better than living paycheck to paycheck, drowning in student loan anxiety, or avoiding your bank account because you're scared to look. You deserve a roadmap that actually makes sense for your life – one that acknowledges you're navigating gig economy jobs, side hustles, student debt, and a completely different financial landscape than your parents did.

Think of this book as a conversation with a financially savvy friend who's been there, made mistakes, learned the hard lessons, and wants to help you skip the painful parts.

We're going to tackle everything from creating a budget that doesn't make you feel deprived to understanding cryptocurrency, building multiple income streams, and yes – even buying your first home.

What makes this book different? Three things: First, it's designed specifically for the adult dealing with 2026 realities – digital banking, cryptocurrency, remote work, and the gig economy. Second, every chapter includes real stories from people who've been exactly where you are now and successfully transformed their financial lives. Third, this book doesn't just tell you what to do; it shows you *how* to do it with practical tools, templates, and step-by-step action plans you can implement immediately.

But here's what I want you to know right now, before we dive in: You don't need to be perfect to start. You don't need a finance degree, a six-figure salary, or a trust fund. You just need to be willing to learn, take action, and commit to your financial future. Every successful person you admire started somewhere, often from a place of financial struggle and uncertainty.

Your financial transformation begins with a single decision to take control. Whether you're starting with debt, zero savings, or just a nagging feeling that you could be doing better with your money, you're in the right place. This book is your companion, your guide, and your roadmap to financial confidence.

So let's get started. Your future self is counting on you, and I promise – you've got this.

Chapter 1. Smart Money Mindset: Building Your Financial Foundation

The influence of our financial mindset reaches far beyond simple dollars and cents. It shapes our career choices, relationships, and even our sense of self-worth. Understanding and reshaping our money mindset is the foundation for building lasting financial success.

Think about it: have you ever felt anxious checking your bank account balance? Do you avoid looking at your credit card statement? Maybe you've caught yourself making an impulse purchase after a stressful day at work, only to feel guilty hours later.

Here's the truth: your current financial situation is not a reflection of your worth or potential. It's simply a starting point. Whether you're drowning in student loan debt, living paycheck to paycheck, or just feeling confused about where your money goes each month, you have the power to change your financial trajectory by first changing how you think about money.

We're going to explore the psychological aspects of money management and provide practical strategies to develop a healthy financial mindset that will serve as the foundation for everything else in this book.

We'll examine common money beliefs and their origins, understand emotional spending triggers, and learn practical strategies to develop positive financial habits.

Most importantly, we'll work on building self-awareness in financial decision-making and provide tools to overcome limiting beliefs about money.

The Psychology of Spending: Emotional Triggers and How to Manage Them

You've had a brutal day at work. Your boss criticized your project, you spilled coffee on your favorite shirt, and you missed lunch because of back-to-back meetings. By the time you're home, you're scrolling through your phone, and suddenly you're checking out with $150 worth of stuff you didn't plan to buy.

Sound familiar? You're not alone, and you're definitely not broken. You've just experienced emotional spending in action.

Here's what's actually happening in your brain: when you make a purchase, your brain releases dopamine, that feel-good chemical that gives you a temporary mood boost. It's the same rush you get from eating chocolate or getting likes on social media.

The problem? That high is fleeting, and it often leaves behind buyer's remorse and a lighter bank account. This "retail therapy" cycle can seriously undermine your financial goals if you don't learn to recognize and manage it.

The tricky part is that emotional spending isn't just triggered by negative feelings. Sure, stress, sadness, and loneliness are major culprits. You're trying to fill an emotional void with material things.

But positive emotions can be just as dangerous. Got a promotion? "I deserve a treat!" Had a great week? "Time to celebrate!" These moments of happiness can lead to overspending just as easily as the tough times, especially when you're riding that emotional high and your guard is down.

Then there's the social pressure factor. Your friends are planning another expensive brunch. Your Instagram feed is filled with people showing off their latest hauls. That influencer you follow just posted a discount code.

Suddenly, you're navigating a minefield of external triggers designed to make you spend. The fear of missing out or not keeping up can push you to make purchases that don't align with your actual values or budget.

So how do you break the cycle? Start with awareness. Keep a simple spending journal for two weeks – not to judge yourself, but to spot patterns. Write down what you bought, how much it cost, and crucially, what you were feeling right before you clicked "buy" or swiped your card.

You'll probably notice trends pretty quickly. Maybe you shop late at night when you're tired. Maybe Sunday evenings trigger spending because you're dreading Monday. Maybe you overspend after talking to a particular friend or scrolling certain apps.

Here's a game-changer: the HALT rule. Never make purchases when you're Hungry, Angry, Lonely, or Tired. These states mess with your decision-making abilities and make you vulnerable to emotional spending. If you catch yourself about to buy something in one of these states, step away. Go for a walk, call a friend, make a snack, or take a nap. Deal with the actual need instead of masking it with a purchase.

Build yourself a "fun money" budget – a specific amount each month that's guilt-free spending for whatever brings you joy. This isn't about deprivation; it's about intention. When you know you have $100 set aside for treats, you can enjoy spending it without derailing your bigger financial goals. The key is sticking to that amount and not letting it creep up every month.

Finally, develop alternative coping strategies for your most common triggers. If stress makes you shop, create a go-to list of free stress relievers: a workout, meditation, journaling, or calling someone who makes you laugh. If celebration triggers overspending, plan low-cost ways to mark wins – a homemade nice dinner, a movie night, or a day trip to somewhere free.

Managing emotional spending is about making conscious choices that support the life you're building, rather than letting temporary feelings dictate your financial future. Your emotions are valid, but they don't have to control your wallet.

The shift starts with one simple practice: track everything for 30 days. Not to shame yourself – just to see. Use an app, a spreadsheet, or even a notebook. The goal is awareness, not judgment. You'll probably spot patterns you didn't realize existed. Maybe you spend more when you're bored. Maybe Friday nights are budget black holes. Maybe those "small" purchases add up to hundreds each month.

Once you see where your money actually goes, it's time to give every dollar a job. This is called zero-based budgeting, and it's a game-changer. Instead of vaguely hoping you'll have money left over at month's end, you assign each dollar a purpose before the month begins: rent, groceries, savings, fun money, whatever. When everything has a job, nothing falls through the cracks.

To protect yourself from impulse buys, add friction to your spending. Remove saved payment info from shopping sites. Unsubscribe from promotional emails. Delete shopping apps from your phone. Then implement the 24-hour rule: wait a full day before buying anything unplanned. For purchases over $100, wait a week. You'll be amazed how many "must-haves" lose their appeal after a cooling-off period.

Remember, this is about progress. Each intentional choice builds on the last, creating habits that compound into real financial freedom. You're directing your resources toward the life you actually want to build. And that? That's powerful.

Setting SMART Financial Goals: The Foundation of Wealth Building

Here's the truth about financial goals: most people set them, get excited for about a week, and then watch them quietly fade into the background noise of daily life. Sound familiar? You're not failing at money – you're just missing a framework that actually works. Enter SMART goals, a system that transforms vague wishes like "save more money" into concrete plans you can actually execute.

SMART stands for Specific, Measurable, Achievable, Relevant, and Time-bound. Originally developed for management objectives, this framework has become the gold standard for personal finance because it eliminates guesswork and creates a clear roadmap you can follow.

Let's break down what each component means for your money and why it matters.

Specific means defining exactly what you want and why. Instead of "I want to save money," try "I want to save $5,000 for a car down payment." See the difference? The second version gives your brain something concrete to work toward. When your goal has a clear purpose, you're far more likely to stick with it when temptation strikes.

Measurable gives you a way to track progress and know when you've won. If you're saving $5,000, that means setting aside roughly $209 per month over two years. This measurability creates feedback loops – you can check in monthly and see yourself getting closer, which fuels motivation way better than hoping you're making progress.

Achievable is where many people stumble. Yes, aim high, but setting a goal to save $10,000 in six months on a $35,000 salary is a setup for failure and frustration. Look at your actual income, expenses, and obligations. What can you realistically commit to without burning out? Maybe $150 per month is your sweet spot right now, and that's perfectly fine. You can always increase it later.

Relevant ensures your goal actually matters to you and fits your bigger picture. Ask yourself: why does this goal matter? How does it align with my values and life plans? If you're focused on building an emergency fund but your friend is investing aggressively, that doesn't mean you're doing it wrong. Your goals should reflect your priorities and current situation, not someone else's Instagram highlight reel.

Time-bound creates urgency and prevents endless procrastination. "Someday I'll save for a vacation" becomes "I'll save $2,000 for a trip in 18 months by contributing $111 per month." That deadline focuses your efforts and helps you plan around it.

Here's a realistic set of SMART goals for your first year: build a $1,500 emergency fund in 10 months, eliminate $1,000 in credit card debt within 12 months by adding $100 to your minimum payment, and save $2,400 for irregular expenses like car repairs or gifts by setting aside $200 monthly. Pick one or two to start – trying to tackle everything at once is a recipe for goal overload.

The beauty of SMART goals is they grow with you. As you knock out your first emergency fund, you'll set a new goal for three months of expenses. As you eliminate credit card debt, you'll redirect that payment toward investing. Each completed goal builds confidence and momentum for the next one, creating a compound effect that transforms your entire financial life.

Breaking Through Money Blocks: Overcoming Financial Fears and Limiting Beliefs

Here's something nobody tells you when you're starting out: the biggest obstacle between you and financial success probably isn't your income, your student loans, or even your spending habits. It's the invisible beliefs that experts call "money blocks," and they're quietly sabotaging your financial decisions every single day.

Money blocks are those deeply ingrained, often subconscious beliefs that shape how you earn, spend, save, and invest. Maybe you freeze up when it's time to negotiate your salary. Maybe you sabotage yourself with impulse purchases right after getting paid. Maybe you avoid looking at your bank account altogether because the anxiety feels overwhelming.

These aren't character flaws – they're learned patterns, usually absorbed during childhood, that now run on autopilot in your adult life.[1]

Think about the money messages you heard growing up. "Money doesn't grow on trees." "Rich people are greedy." "We can't afford that." "Don't talk about money – it's rude." Each of these seemingly innocent phrases planted seeds that grew into your current money mindset.

If your parents constantly stressed about bills, you might have internalized a scarcity belief – that there will never be enough, no matter how much you earn. If money was never discussed, you probably feel uncomfortable talking about your salary or asking friends for financial advice. These early experiences create patterns that follow you into every financial decision you make today.

The tricky part? Money blocks show up differently for everyone. Some people hoard every penny out of fear, even when they're financially stable. Others spend impulsively the moment money hits their account, as if it'll disappear if they don't use it immediately. Some avoid investing because they're terrified of losing money, while others feel guilty about having more than their friends or family. You might even recognize the feast-or-famine cycle – oscillating between extreme restriction and excessive spending, never finding a sustainable middle ground.

So how do you actually break through these blocks? Start with awareness. Grab a notebook and spend fifteen minutes answering these questions honestly:

- What did your family teach you about money?

- When do you feel most anxious about finances?

- What patterns keep repeating in your financial life?

- Do your spending habits actually reflect your values, or someone else's expectations?

Once you've identified your specific blocks, it's time to challenge them. For every limiting belief you uncover, write down evidence that contradicts it. If you believe "I'm just bad with money," counter it with times you made smart financial choices – even small ones count. Replace "I'll never be able to afford that" with "I'm creating a plan to make that possible." This is about replacing limiting beliefs with empowering truths that actually serve your goals.

Listen, overcoming money blocks is an ongoing practice of noticing patterns, challenging beliefs, and making intentional choices that align with the life you're building. Celebrate the small wins – checking your account regularly, making your first investment, saying no to a purchase that doesn't serve your goals. Each of these victories rewires your relationship with money from one of fear or avoidance to one of confidence and capability.

Your money blocks are real, but they're not permanent. With awareness, intention, and consistent practice, you can transform the invisible scripts running your financial life and finally take control of your money story.

Creating Your Personal Money Philosophy: Values-Based Financial Planning

Here's a question most financial advice skips right over: *Why* do you want money in the first place?

Not the surface answer – "to pay bills" or "to be comfortable" – but the deeper truth. What kind of future are you actually trying to build?

Your answer to that question is the foundation of what financial experts call values-based financial planning, and it's the difference between a budget that feels like a straitjacket and a money plan that actually excites you.

Traditional financial planning starts with numbers: how much you earn, how much you owe, how much you should save. Values-based planning flips that script entirely. It starts with *you* – what matters most, what you're working toward, what kind of person you want to be – and then builds your financial strategy around those core truths. It leads to better follow-through and more sustainable financial habits because your money choices connect to something deeper than arbitrary rules.

Think about it this way: if security is one of your core values, you'll naturally prioritize a solid emergency fund and conservative debt levels. If freedom ranks high, you might focus on building multiple income streams and keeping your fixed expenses low so you have flexibility to pivot when opportunities arise. If contribution matters most to you, you'll weave charitable giving and sustainable investing into your plan from day one. None of these is "right" or "wrong" – they're just different reflections of different values.

So how do you actually build your personal money philosophy? Start by identifying your top three to five core values. These are the principles that genuinely drive your decisions when the stakes are high.

Reflect on moments when you felt most fulfilled, people you deeply admire, and situations that consistently frustrate you. Those reactions reveal what you truly prize. Common values include security, freedom, growth, family, creativity, adventure, and impact. Your combination is uniquely yours.

Once you've named your values, translate them into concrete financial strategies. This is where values stop being abstract concepts and start shaping real decisions.

If growth is essential, allocate resources to courses, certifications, and tools that enhance your earning power. If family is central, prioritize life insurance and create space in your budget for quality time together. If adventure calls to you, build a dedicated travel fund and structure your work to allow for flexibility.

Now create your money rules – five to seven specific guidelines that operationalize your values into daily behavior. These become your decision-making shortcuts when temptation strikes or choices feel overwhelming.

Examples:

- Always contribute enough to get the full employer match.
- Wait 48 hours before any purchase over $100.
- Automatically direct 5% of income to causes I believe in.
- Never carry a credit card balance that charges interest.

Write these down and revisit them before major financial decisions.

You can also implement "value buckets" for your budget. Instead of generic categories, allocate your income to buckets that reflect what matters most – essentials, future security, freedom fund, personal growth, relationships, and impact.

This method makes trade-offs explicit. When you're deciding between a weekend trip and extra debt payments, you're not just comparing numbers; you're asking which choice better honors your stated values.

You might want to write a brief personal money philosophy statement that captures your values and rules in one paragraph. Example: "I value security, freedom, and contribution. I will maintain a six-month emergency fund, invest 15% of income in diversified low-cost portfolios, avoid high-interest debt, give 5% to causes I believe in, and review my plan quarterly."

Keep it visible. Reference it when making decisions. Let it guide you back to center when external pressures pull you off course. It's about creating a financial life that reflects who you are and what you're building, and that alignment is what makes lasting financial success possible.

As we wrap up this first chapter, I want you to take a moment and really let this sink in: your relationship with money isn't something you're just "good at" or "bad at" like some genetic trait you inherited. It's a skill you can develop, a mindset you can reshape, and a story you can rewrite starting right now.

Here's what I need you to understand: this work isn't glamorous. Nobody's going to throw you a party when you implement your first 24-hour waiting period or write down your personal money philosophy. But these small, unglamorous actions? They build on each other and create momentum that eventually transforms your entire financial life.

So here's your challenge as you move forward: pick one thing from this chapter – just one – and implement it this week. Maybe it's journaling about your money story for fifteen minutes. Maybe it's setting up that weekly money date with yourself. Maybe it's writing down your first SMART financial goal or creating your personal money philosophy statement. Don't try to do everything at once. Start small, build momentum, and let success breed more success.

In the next chapter, we're diving into the practical world of digital banking and modern money management tools – the systems that will help you automate and streamline everything we've discussed here. But those tools only work if you've built the foundation we've established in this chapter. Your mindset is the soil; everything else is what grows from it.

You've taken the first step. That's the hardest one. Now let's keep building.

Chapter 2. Digital Banking Mastery: Modern Tools for Money Management

Have you ever felt that moment of panic when you're not sure if a bill payment went through, or wondered if that suspicious charge on your account is legitimate? Online banking has transformed these anxious moments into simple, quick checks you can do from anywhere.

But here's the thing – most people barely scratch the surface of what their online banking platform can do, missing out on features that could save them hours each month and hundreds of dollars in fees.

Let me walk you through what makes online banking so powerful and how to use it safely. Think of your online banking platform as your financial command center – it's where you can see everything happening with your money in real-time, not days later when a paper statement arrives.

When I first started using online banking seriously, I was amazed to discover I could see pending transactions immediately, which meant I could actually prevent overdrafts instead of just discovering them after the fact.

The Features That Actually Matter

The most valuable feature of online banking is 24/7 account visibility with real-time updates. Instead of guessing whether you can afford that dinner out, you know exactly where you stand. According to recent data, 77 percent of consumers now prefer managing their bank accounts digitally, with millennials leading at 80 percent adoption.

Mobile check deposit is another game-changer. To use this feature, simply open your banking app, select "deposit check," take photos of the front and back, and confirm the amount. Most checks are available within one business day.

We'll get into this more in a bit, but bill pay and automated transfers are where online banking really shines for preventing costly mistakes. I recommend setting up automatic payments for fixed bills like rent and insurance, while keeping variable expenses like utilities on manual payment with alert reminders.

Mobile Payment Solutions: Digital Wallets and Peer-to-Peer Payments

Have you ever been out to dinner with friends, split the bill, and then spent the next week trying to track down who still owes you money? Or maybe you've stood in line at a coffee shop, fumbling through your wallet for the right card while everyone behind you waits impatiently.

These everyday frustrations are exactly why digital wallets and peer-to-peer payment apps have become essential tools for managing money in 2026. They're not just convenient – they're transforming how we think about and handle transactions in our daily lives.

Let me be clear about what we're talking about here. Digital wallets are secure apps on your phone that store your payment information, letting you pay for things with just a tap or click. Instead of carrying physical cards, your payment details are converted into secure digital tokens that protect your actual card numbers. Think of it as your physical wallet's smarter, safer cousin that lives in your phone and never gets left on the bus.

The real magic happens when you understand how these tools actually work for you. When you tap your phone at a checkout terminal, your digital wallet uses something called NFC (near-field communication) technology to securely transmit a one-time code – not your actual card number – to complete the purchase.

This tokenization means that even if someone intercepted that transaction data, they couldn't use it to steal from you. Your phone also requires biometric authentication – your fingerprint or face – before authorizing the payment, adding another layer of security that your physical wallet simply can't match.

Here's where it gets practical for your everyday life. The main players you'll encounter are Apple Pay, Google Pay, and Samsung Pay for contactless payments, plus apps like Venmo, Cash App, and Zelle for sending money to friends.

I personally use Google Pay for almost all my in-store purchases and Venmo for splitting costs with friends, and the time I've saved is crazy. No more ATM trips to get cash for splitting Uber rides or concert tickets.

Setting Up Your First Digital Wallet

Ready to get started? Here's exactly what to do.

- First, open the wallet app that came with your phone – it's already installed on most devices.

- Tap "Add Card" and either scan your card with your camera or type in the details manually. Your bank will verify the card, usually by sending a text code to confirm it's really you.

- Enable biometric authentication in your phone's security settings – this is non-negotiable for keeping your money safe.

- Finally, start small: buy a coffee or lunch using tap-to-pay to get comfortable with the process before using it for larger purchases.

For peer-to-peer payments, download your preferred app, link your bank account or debit card, and verify your identity. Most apps require identity verification to unlock higher sending limits, so have your driver's license handy.

One crucial tip I learned the hard way: always double-check the recipient before hitting send! Unlike traditional banking, P2P payments are often instant and irreversible.

The Real Benefits for Your Financial Life

Beyond convenience, these tools offer surprising advantages for managing your money. Most digital wallets automatically categorize your spending, giving you instant insights into where your money actually goes. I discovered I was spending nearly $200 monthly on food delivery, and seeing that number in my wallet's analytics motivated me to cut back immediately.

Many platforms also integrate loyalty programs automatically, so you're earning rewards without carrying physical cards or remembering to scan anything.

The security features alone make digital payments worth adopting. You can instantly freeze your card through the app if something seems suspicious, and you'll receive real-time alerts for every transaction. When my card number was stolen last year, I caught the fraudulent charge within minutes because of these alerts – something that would have taken days to discover with traditional banking.

One word of caution: while these tools are incredibly secure, you still need to maintain good habits. Keep your phone's operating system updated, never share your login credentials, and review your transactions weekly. The technology protects you, but your vigilance completes the security picture.

Finding Your Perfect Budgeting Match

The secret to sticking with a budgeting app is choosing one that matches your personality and financial style. If you're someone who wants complete control and doesn't mind being hands-on, YNAB (You Need A Budget) might be your perfect fit. It uses a "give every dollar a job" strategy that forces you to plan ahead and prioritize savings. Think of it as the personal trainer of budgeting apps – it pushes you, but you'll see results if you commit.

Prefer something more automated? Mint connects to your bank accounts and credit cards, automatically categorizing your transactions and alerting you when you're overspending in a category. I recommend this for beginners who want structure without the daily maintenance. The app does the heavy lifting while you focus on making better decisions based on the insights it provides.

For spreadsheet lovers who want automation without sacrificing control, Tiller is a game-changer. It feeds your transaction data directly into Google Sheets or Excel templates that you can customize however you want. You get daily balance updates and complete transparency – perfect if you're the type who likes to see the formulas behind the numbers.

If you want something simple to start, try Monarch Money's "Flex" budget system, which divides spending into just three buckets: fixed expenses, non-monthly recurring costs, and flexible spending. This removes the intimidation factor while still giving you control.

Now, if you're building wealth while managing daily expenses, you need something more comprehensive. Empower (formerly Personal Capital) gives you a unified dashboard that tracks both your spending *and* your investment portfolios across multiple institutions. A certified financial planner specifically recommends this for new investors because it shows your complete financial picture – checking accounts, credit cards, 401(k)s, even 529 plans – all in one place. This becomes invaluable as your financial life grows more complex.

Cybersecurity Essentials: Protecting Your Digital Financial Life

Let me ask you something: Have you ever gotten that sinking feeling when you see an unfamiliar charge on your account, or received a text claiming your bank account has been "compromised" and you need to click a link immediately?

If your heart rate just sped up reading that, you're not alone. Cybercriminals are counting on that panic response – and we are their favorite targets.

Here's the uncomfortable truth: We're prime targets not because we're careless, but because we live our entire financial lives online. We bank on our phones, split dinner bills through Venmo, and shop on public Wi-Fi at coffee shops. Every digital transaction creates an opportunity for someone with bad intentions. But before you decide to go back to cash and paper statements, let me show you how to protect yourself without giving up the convenience that makes digital banking so powerful.

The Real Threats You're Facing

The cybercriminals targeting your money aren't the hoodie-wearing hackers from movies – they're sophisticated operations using psychology as much as technology. Account takeover is their favorite play: they steal your login credentials through phishing emails or fake websites, then drain your account or use it as a steppingstone to access your other financial accounts. I've seen friends lose thousands because they clicked one convincing fake email that looked exactly like it came from their bank.

Then there's the SIM swap attack – criminals convince your phone carrier to transfer your number to their device, intercepting the text codes your bank sends for verification. Suddenly, they're you, at least as far as your bank's security system knows. Card fraud, malicious apps, and social engineering scams round out the threat landscape, and they're all more common than you think.

Your Essential Security Playbook

Here's what you need to do today – not tomorrow, today. First, enable multi-factor authentication (MFA) on every financial account you own. Open your banking app right now, go to security settings, and turn on MFA. Choose app-based authentication like Google Authenticator or your bank's proprietary app over SMS codes whenever possible – remember those SIM swap attacks? Yes, it adds an extra step when you log in, but that extra step is the difference between your money staying yours and becoming someone else's.

Next, get a password manager and use it religiously. I know, I know, another app to manage. But here's why it matters: using "Summer2024!" for both your bank and your email means one breach compromises everything. A password manager creates unique, complex passwords for each account and remembers them for you. I use one, and it's saved me from myself more times than I can count.

The Habits That Keep You Safe

Never – and I mean never – access your bank account on public Wi-Fi without a VPN. That free airport Wi-Fi? It's a playground for criminals intercepting your data. Use your phone's cellular data instead, or invest in a reputable VPN service if you travel frequently.

Keep your phone's operating system and apps updated. Those annoying update notifications? They're patching security vulnerabilities that criminals actively exploit. Enable automatic updates and let your phone protect itself while you sleep.

Finally, trust your instincts. If you receive an email or text claiming there's a problem with your account, don't click any links. Open your banking app directly or call the number on the back of your card. Your bank will never ask you to verify your password through email or text – that's always a scam.

Spend thirty minutes today implementing these protections, and you'll have peace of mind for years to come. Your future self will thank you.

Automated Financial Management: Bill Pay, Recurring Transfers, and Alerts

It's the 15th of the month, you're swamped at work, and suddenly you remember – did you pay your electric bill? You scramble to check, praying you didn't just get hit with a late fee.

Now imagine never having that panic again. That's the power of automation, and it's about to become your new best friend.

When you automate your bill payments, recurring transfers, and alerts, you're essentially hiring a 24/7 assistant who never forgets a due date, never sleeps through a payday, and always has your back. According to recent data, 39% of consumers now use automatic payments for recurring bills, and that number keeps climbing because automation simply works.

Let me walk you through exactly how to set this up so you can start sleeping better tonight. First, let's tackle automated bill payments.

Log into your bank's website or app and look for "Bill Pay" or "Payments" in the main menu. You'll see an option to add a payee – this is where you enter the company you're paying, like your landlord or utility provider.

Here's my strategy: automate *everything* that's the same amount every month. Rent? Automate it. Car payment? Automate it. Netflix subscription? Definitely automate it.

For bills that vary each month, like credit cards or utilities, I recommend a hybrid approach that's saved me countless times. Set up automatic payments for the *minimum* amount due, which protects your credit score if you forget to pay.44 45 Then, manually pay the remaining balance after reviewing your statement each month. This way, you're protected from late fees while still maintaining oversight of variable expenses.

Now here's where automation gets really exciting – recurring transfers for savings. Open your banking app and find "Transfers" or "Move Money." Set up an automatic transfer from your checking to your savings account that happens the day after each paycheck hits. Start small if you need to – even $50 per paycheck adds up to $1,300 per year.

The beauty of "pay yourself first" is that you never see the money in your checking account, so you're not tempted to spend it. I started with just $75 per paycheck three years ago, and my emergency fund now sits at $6,000 without me consciously thinking about it.

Here's your action plan for this week: Pick your three most important fixed bills and automate them today. Set up one recurring transfer to savings that happens after your next paycheck. Enable at least three account alerts. That's it.

Digital Banking Red Flags: Avoiding Scams and Fraud

Have you ever received a text claiming your bank account has been "locked for suspicious activity" and you need to click a link immediately to verify your identity? That split-second panic is exactly what scammers are counting on – and unfortunately, we are their favorite targets.

Here's the uncomfortable truth: despite being digital natives, Gen Z users are more than three times as likely to fall victim to online scams compared to Baby Boomers. It's not because we're careless – it's because we live our entire financial lives online, creating countless opportunities for criminals to strike.

Nearly one-third of adults aged 18-34 report being victimized by financial scams, with job scams, investment fraud, and fake check schemes topping the list. As Sophia Leung from TD Bank puts it, "Growing up as a digital native and being more technologically savvy doesn't mean you're immune to the dangers of online scams."

So what should you actually watch for? Let me walk you through the red flags that should make you stop and think twice before clicking, sending money, or sharing information.

The Red Flags That Scream "Scam"

First, any unsolicited message claiming there's a problem with your account requiring immediate action is suspect. Real banks don't operate this way. If Chase or Bank of America needs to reach you about a genuine issue, they'll send a secure message through your banking app or call from a verified number – never through a random text with a suspicious link.

Watch out for requests for sensitive information like passwords, one-time verification codes, or your full account number through text, email, or social media. I'll say this plainly: your bank will *never* ask for these details through unsecured channels. Not ever. If someone claiming to be from your bank asks for your one-time passcode, hang up immediately – they're trying to break into your account while you're on the phone.

Payment demands are another massive red flag. If someone insists you pay via gift cards, cryptocurrency, wire transfer, or peer-to-peer apps like Venmo to someone you don't know personally, that's a scam. Legitimate businesses and government agencies don't accept iTunes gift cards as payment. Period.

Then there are the too-good-to-be-true offers – investment opportunities promising guaranteed high returns, job offers that require you to pay upfront for "training materials," or online deals that seem impossibly cheap. Last year, my roommate nearly fell for a "remote job" that would have paid $3,000 weekly for data entry. The catch? She needed to send $200 for equipment first. That $200 would have disappeared forever.

What To Do Right Now

Here's your action plan for protecting yourself today. First, verify before you act. If you receive any message about your account, don't click links or call numbers provided in the message. Instead, open your banking app directly or call the number printed on the back of your card. This simple step stops most scams cold.

Second, never share one-time verification codes with anyone, even someone claiming to be from your bank's fraud department. Those codes are the keys to your account – sharing them is like handing over your house keys to a stranger.

Third, keep your social media profiles private and think carefully about what you post. Scammers mine social media for personal details like your birthday, pet's name, or hometown, which can help them answer security questions or make their impersonation more convincing.

If You've Been Targeted

If you suspect fraud, act immediately.

- Stop all contact with the suspected scammer and don't send any money or information.
- Take screenshots of messages and record any phone numbers or usernames.
- Contact your bank right away to lock your cards and freeze your accounts.

- Change your passwords, starting with your email, and enable two-factor authentication everywhere.

The bottom line? Scammers are sophisticated, but they rely on you acting quickly without thinking. Slow down, verify independently, and trust your instincts. If something feels off, it probably is. Your financial security is worth the extra two minutes it takes to double-check.

Here's what I really want you to remember: digital banking tools are only as effective as your willingness to stay engaged with them. Yes, automation is powerful, but you still need those weekly fifteen-minute money dates to review your transactions, adjust your budget, and catch any issues early.

Think of it like this – automation is your financial assistant, but you're still the boss. You need to check in regularly to make sure everything's running smoothly.

The digital banking landscape will continue evolving, with new apps, features, and technologies emerging regularly. Stay curious and open to learning, but always evaluate new tools with the security-first mindset we've discussed. Not every new app or platform is worth adopting – choose tools that genuinely solve problems in your financial life and align with your goals.

Chapter 3. The Budget Blueprint: Creating a Sustainable Spending Plan

Are you tired of feeling like your money controls you instead of the other way around? If you've ever reached the end of the month wondering where your paycheck went, you're not alone.

The reality is that most of us face unique financial challenges that traditional budgeting methods don't fully address. With the rise of the gig economy, variable income streams, and digital payment platforms making it easier than ever to spend without thinking, we need a fresh look at money management that actually fits our modern lifestyle.

Think about it – your grandparents might have balanced a checkbook and paid bills with paper checks. Your parents probably used spreadsheets and online banking. But in 2026, you're juggling Venmo payments, subscription services that auto-renew, and side hustles that deposit money at irregular intervals. Traditional budgeting advice simply wasn't designed for this reality.

As we explore the various budgeting strategies and tools in this chapter, remember that the goal is to create a personalized money management system that gives you clarity, control, and confidence in your financial decisions. Whether you're working a traditional job or hustling in the gig economy, these principles can be adapted to fit your unique situation.

Let's begin by examining the fundamental building blocks of a budget that actually works for your lifestyle.

The 50/30/20 Rule: Adapting Traditional Budgeting for Modern Life

Have you ever wondered if there's a simpler way to budget without tracking every single dollar? Let me introduce you to one of the most practical frameworks that's helping people take control of their money: the 50/30/20 rule. This divides what you actually take home (after taxes) into three straightforward categories: 50% for needs, 30% for wants, and 20% for savings and debt payoff.

Here's what each bucket means in real life:

Needs (50%): Your must-haves – rent, groceries, utilities, car payment, insurance, and minimum debt payments

Wants (30%): Everything that makes life enjoyable – dining out, Netflix, concerts, new clothes, that daily latte

Savings and Debt (20%): Your future self – emergency fund, retirement accounts, and extra payments on loans

What makes this rule so powerful in 2026 is its flexibility. Unlike rigid budgets that make you feel guilty for every purchase, this framework gives you permission to enjoy life while still building wealth. Think of it as financial guardrails rather than a financial prison.

Let's be honest – if you're living in New York, San Francisco, or any high-cost city, your rent alone might eat up 40% of your income. Does that mean this rule won't work for you? Absolutely not. You might need to adjust to 60/20/20 temporarily while you work on increasing your income or finding ways to reduce housing costs. The percentages are targets, not commandments carved in stone.

Here's how to actually implement this in your life. First, figure out your take-home pay – that's what hits your bank account after taxes and deductions. If you're freelancing or have a side hustle, remember to set aside money for taxes first, then apply the rule to what's left. Open your banking app right now and look at last month's deposits. That's your starting number.

Next, categorize your spending. This is where modern banking apps become your best friend. Most apps now automatically sort your transactions into categories. Spend ten minutes reviewing last month and labeling anything the app got wrong. You'll quickly see where your money actually goes versus where you think it goes – and trust me, there's usually a gap.

One mistake I see constantly: people classify wants as needs. Your basic phone plan? That's a need. Upgrading to the latest iPhone every year? That's a want. Groceries for home cooking? Need. Uber Eats three times a week? Want. Be brutally honest with yourself here.

Now here's the game-changing strategy: automate your 20% the moment you get paid. Set up automatic transfers to your savings account and schedule extra debt payments before you have a chance to spend that money. What you don't see, you won't miss. After automating savings and covering your fixed needs, whatever remains is your guilt-free spending money for the month.

What if your income jumps around like a kangaroo on espresso? Welcome to the gig economy reality. Here's your solution: calculate your "baseline income" by averaging your lowest three months of earnings. Build your 50/30/20 budget around that conservative number. When you have a great month and earn extra, funnel that surplus straight into your 20% bucket. This smooths out the feast-or-famine cycle that keeps so many freelancers up at night.

As your income grows – and it will – resist lifestyle inflation. When you get that raise or land a better-paying job, keep living on your current budget and redirect the increase toward savings and debt payoff. This one habit can shave years off your debt repayment and accelerate your path to financial freedom.

Starting with high student loans or an entry-level salary? Don't let perfect be the enemy of good. Begin with 5% savings if that's all you can manage, then increase it by one or two percentage points every few months.

Digital Expense Tracking: Tools and Techniques for Real-Time Money Management

Money has a sneaky way of disappearing when you're not watching. The good news? In 2026, tracking every dollar doesn't mean drowning in receipts or wrestling with complicated spreadsheets. Modern expense tracking tools do the heavy lifting for you, giving

you instant visibility into your spending the moment you swipe, tap,
or click.

Here's why real-time tracking changes everything: when you see that
$47 restaurant charge pop up on your phone minutes after dinner,
you immediately know how much "fun money" you have left for the
week. That instant feedback loop helps you pump the brakes before
overspending, not after you've already blown your budget. It's like
having a financial coach in your pocket, minus the judgment.

Building Your Digital Tracking System

Start by linking all your financial accounts – checking, savings,
credit cards, even that old student loan – to create one unified
dashboard. Think of it as your financial command center. Instead of
logging into five different apps to figure out where you stand, you
see everything in one place: your net worth, monthly spending by
category, and exactly how much you can safely spend today.

Most tracking apps use artificial intelligence to sort your
transactions into categories. That $8.50 charge at Starbucks?
Automatically tagged as "Coffee & Dining." Your Netflix
subscription? Filed under "Entertainment."

During your first few weeks, you'll need to correct some mistakes.
Maybe the app thinks your gym membership is "Shopping" instead
of "Health & Fitness." But the app learns from your corrections and
gets smarter over time.

Set up alerts that actually matter to you. Low balance warnings
prevent overdraft fees. Large purchase notifications catch fraudulent
charges immediately. Bill-due reminders stop late fees before they
happen. One user I know sets a weekly spending digest that arrives
every Sunday morning – it's become part of her coffee routine and
gives her a clear picture before the week begins.

Choosing Your Tools

Empower Personal Dashboard gives you the big picture for free –
spending, net worth, and you can even share access with your
partner or roommate. Quicken Simplifi works great if you're just

starting out and want something that holds your hand with clear visuals and personalized plans. Love spreadsheets? Tiller automatically feeds your bank data into Google Sheets or Excel every day, giving you total control to customize however you want.

For side hustlers and freelancers, add a receipt-scanning app like Zoho Expense to your toolkit. Snap a photo of that business lunch receipt, and the app reads it, categorizes it, and stores it for tax time. No more shoebox full of crumpled receipts or that panicked scramble in April trying to remember what that $83 charge from six months ago was for.

One final truth: automation is powerful, but it's not perfect. Apps occasionally misread merchants or miss duplicate charges. That weekly review catches these hiccups before they snowball. Think of your tracking system as a partnership – the app does the grunt work, but you're still the boss making the final decisions.

The goal isn't tracking for tracking's sake. It's because when you know exactly where your money goes, you stop wondering why you're always broke and start making intentional choices that align with what you actually value. That's when budgeting stops feeling like restriction and starts feeling like freedom.

Variable Income Budgeting: Strategies for Gig Economy Workers and Freelancers

If your income changes every month, traditional budgeting advice can feel like trying to fit a square peg into a round hole. One month you're celebrating a $5,000 payday, the next you're scraping by on $2,200. Sound familiar? Whether you're driving for Uber, freelancing as a graphic designer, or juggling multiple gig economy jobs, you need a budgeting system built for your reality.

Here's the truth that most budgeting books won't tell you: the feast-or-famine cycle isn't a personal failure. It's the nature of variable income work. And you have it in you to design a financial system that smooths out the bumps and protects you during lean months.

Your Baseline Number: The Foundation of Everything

Stop budgeting based on your best month. Seriously, stop. That's the fastest path to financial chaos. Instead, pull up your bank statements from the last six to twelve months and calculate your average monthly income. Better yet, identify your lowest-earning month in that period. This becomes your baseline – the conservative income figure you'll build your entire budget around.

Let's say your income over the past year ranged from $2,400 to $5,200, averaging around $3,750. Your baseline should be somewhere between $2,400 and $3,500 – not the $5,200 you earned that one amazing month. This guarantees you can cover essentials even when work slows down.

The Self-Paycheck System: Your Income Smoother

Here's the game-changing strategy that transformed my clients' financial lives: treat yourself like an employee. Open a separate savings account – call it your "holding account" – and route all your gig income there first. Every payment from every client, every platform, every side hustle goes into this account.

Then, on the 1st and 15th of each month (or whatever dates work for you), transfer your fixed baseline amount to your regular checking account. That's your "paycheck." Pay your bills, buy groceries, and live your life from this checking account. The surplus sitting in your holding account? That's your buffer for slow months, tax payments, and emergencies.

This system does something magical: it removes the emotional rollercoaster of variable income. You're no longer rich on Tuesday and broke by Friday. You have predictable, steady cash flow even though your actual earnings fluctuate wildly.

Prioritize Like Your Financial Life Depends On It (Because It Does)

Create three spending tiers in your budget:

Essential (Tier 1): Rent, utilities, minimum debt payments, basic groceries, insurance, and taxes – these get paid first, always

Important (Tier 2): Phone plan, internet, transportation costs, professional development

Nice-to-Have (Tier 3): Dining out, entertainment, subscriptions, new clothes

During strong months, you enjoy all three tiers. When income dips, you immediately cut Tier 3 and possibly scale back Tier 2. This prioritization system gives you a clear action plan instead of panicking about what to cut.

The Tax Account: Non-Negotiable

Open a third account exclusively for taxes. The moment any payment hits your holding account, immediately transfer 25-30% to your tax account. Treat this like a bill you cannot skip. Come tax time, you'll have the cash ready instead of scrambling or going into debt to pay the IRS.

Your Action Plan This Week

- First, calculate your baseline using your lowest or average income from recent months.

- Second, list your essential monthly expenses – the absolute minimum you need to survive. If essentials exceed your baseline, you have two choices: cut costs or increase your income floor.

- Third, open those separate accounts if you haven't already: holding, operating, and tax savings.

- Fourth, set up automatic transfers for your self-paycheck and tax set-asides.

- Finally, during your next high-earning month, resist lifestyle inflation. Funnel that surplus into your buffer until you have at least three months of baseline income saved.

Variable income doesn't mean variable financial security. With the right system, you can build stability even when your paychecks refuse to cooperate. The key is planning for the worst months while saving aggressively during the best ones.

Lifestyle Design: Balancing Essential Expenses with Quality of Life

What if I told you that building wealth doesn't mean living like a monk? Here's the truth most personal finance gurus won't admit: budgets that make you miserable don't work. You'll white-knuckle it for three months, then blow everything on a shopping spree because you feel deprived.

The secret isn't choosing between financial security and actually enjoying your life – it's designing a lifestyle that delivers both.

Think of lifestyle design as your personal money blueprint. Instead of defaulting to what everyone else does or mindlessly upgrading every time you get a raise, you're making intentional choices about what truly matters to you. Research shows that financial stress tanks both your mental and physical health, but here's the flip side: budgets that ignore joy create what experts call "budget fatigue," and you'll abandon them faster than a New Year's gym membership.

Your Essential Expenses: The Non-Negotiables

Start with your foundation – the expenses you absolutely cannot skip. Housing, transportation, food, insurance, debt payments, and your emergency fund. These are your financial guardrails. A common benchmark suggests keeping total fixed costs below 50% of your take-home pay, giving you breathing room when life throws curveballs.

Let's talk housing. The old rule says spend no more than 30% of your income on rent. But what if you're in Seattle or Austin where rents are insane? Here's where smart trade-offs come in. Maybe you pay slightly more to live near work, eliminating a soul-crushing two-hour commute and a car payment. Studies consistently show that long commutes destroy life satisfaction and health – sometimes paying more for location actually improves your financial position.

Transportation is your second-biggest money pit. The real cost of owning a car – depreciation, insurance, gas, repairs – often doubles what you think you're paying. Before you finance that new SUV, run the numbers on alternatives. Could you bike? Use public transit? Share a car with your roommate? One less car can free up hundreds monthly for goals that actually matter to you.

Quality of Life: The Spending That Fuels You

Now here's where it gets interesting. Research proves that spending on experiences – concerts, weekend trips, cooking classes with friends – delivers more lasting happiness than buying stuff. That new gaming console gives you a quick dopamine hit, but the memories from a camping trip with your best friends? Those compound over time.

Protect what researchers call your "joy line items." Maybe it's your climbing gym membership, your monthly book budget, or Sunday brunch with friends. These aren't frivolous – they're the spending that keeps you sane and motivated. Cut these and you'll sabotage your entire financial plan.

Here's a framework that actually works: identify your top three to five values. Is it adventure? Learning? Community? Health? Now look at your spending. Does your money reflect those values, or are you hemorrhaging cash on things you don't actually care about? This "values-to-dollars map" becomes your decision-making filter.

Making It Sustainable

Implement a "raise rule" right now. When your income increases, automatically route 50% to savings and debt before upgrading anything. This single habit prevents lifestyle creep – that sneaky phenomenon where your spending magically rises to match every raise, leaving you perpetually broke at higher income levels.

Set up what financial planners call sinking funds – separate savings for predictable irregular expenses like car insurance, annual subscriptions, or holiday gifts. This prevents you from raiding your emergency fund or reaching for a credit card when these bills arrive.

When you intentionally design your lifestyle around what truly matters, budgeting stops feeling like deprivation and starts feeling like freedom.

Building Your Money Highway: The Hub-and-Spoke System

Picture your checking account as a traffic hub where money arrives, then immediately routes to different destinations. Your paycheck lands in checking (the hub), then automatically splits into various "spokes" – savings accounts, investment accounts, and bill payments. This structure ensures every dollar knows exactly where it's going without you playing traffic cop.

Here's your setup checklist:

- Contact HR and split your direct deposit: route percentages to different accounts the moment you get paid

- Open a high-yield savings account for your emergency fund (look for 4%+ interest rates in 2026)

- Create separate savings "buckets" for specific goals – vacation, car maintenance, annual insurance premiums

- Enable automatic bill pay for fixed expenses like rent, phone, internet, and subscriptions

- Schedule recurring investment transfers to happen on payday, not at month's end

The "Pay Yourself First" Revolution

Most people save whatever's left after spending. Spoiler alert: there's never anything left. Flip the script. The moment your paycheck hits, automation whisks away your savings and investment contributions before you can spend it. Behavioral finance research proves that automatic enrollment and escalation in savings plans dramatically increase both participation rates and long-term wealth accumulation. What you don't see, you won't miss.

Start with your employer's 401(k) if available. Set contributions to at least capture the full company match – that's literally free money. Then enable the auto-escalation feature that bumps your contribution by 1% annually. You won't even notice the gradual increase, but your future self will thank you.

Debt Destruction on Autopilot

Set up automatic minimum payments for every debt you have – student loans, credit cards, car loans, everything. This single move protects your credit score since payment history accounts for the largest chunk of your credit score. Many student loan servicers even reward you with a 0.25% interest rate reduction just for enrolling in autopay.

But don't stop at minimums. Schedule a second automatic payment toward your highest-interest debt, following the debt avalanche method. Let's say you have $300 extra monthly for debt payoff. Automate $300 to your credit card with the 22% APR while minimums handle everything else. When that card's gone, redirect that $300 to the next highest-rate debt without thinking about it.

Your Safety Net: Essential Safeguards

Automation is powerful, but you need guardrails. Keep a one-month expense buffer in your bill-pay checking account to prevent overdrafts when timing gets wonky. Schedule all transfers and payments for one or two days after your paycheck arrives – never before. Enable low-balance alerts so you catch potential problems before they become expensive mistakes.

Your Monthly Money Check-In: The 15-Minute Habit That Changes Everything

Block fifteen minutes at the end of each month – seriously, put it in your calendar right now. During this session, pull up your banking app and compare what you actually spent versus what you planned to spend. Don't judge yourself; just observe. Did you blow past your grocery budget by $150? That's not failure – that's data telling you to adjust next month's allocation or rethink your shopping strategy.

Here's your monthly checklist:

- Review every transaction and make sure it's categorized correctly

- Identify any category where actual spending exceeded your plan by more than 10%

- Check progress on your savings goals and debt payoff targets

- Update any variable expense categories based on recent price changes

- Confirm all your automated transfers and bill payments processed correctly

- Note one spending pattern you want to change next month

Quarterly Deep Dives: When Life Shifts Gears

Every three months, go deeper to recalibrate your entire financial strategy. Revisit your big-picture goals. Is that emergency fund target still right, or do you need to bump it up because you switched to freelance work? Are you still prioritizing the same debt, or should you redirect extra payments now that interest rates have changed?

Inflation doesn't take breaks, so neither should your budget adjustments. If your grocery bill has crept from $300 to $375 over the past quarter, that's not you failing at budgeting – that's the cost of eggs doubling. Adjust your allocation to match reality, then look for other categories where you can trim to compensate.

The Guardrail System: Automatic Course Corrections

Set up trigger points that force action before small problems become financial emergencies. For example: "If my actual savings rate drops below 15% for two consecutive months, I immediately cut discretionary spending by 20% the following month." Or: "If my credit card balance exceeds $1,000, I pause all non-essential purchases until it's back under $500."

These guardrails remove emotion from tough decisions. You're not depriving yourself – you're following the rules you set when your head was clear and your bank account wasn't screaming.

When Income Jumps Around

Variable income demands more frequent check-ins. Review your baseline income calculation quarterly using your most recent earnings data. If you've had three strong months in a row, you might cautiously raise your baseline slightly – but never budget based on your best month. That's financial fantasy, not planning.

The Annual Reset: Your Financial New Year

Once a year, rebuild your budget from scratch. Recalculate your take-home pay, especially if you got a raise or changed jobs. Review all your insurance coverage – are you still adequately protected? Adjust your retirement contributions, ideally increasing by at least 1%. Plan for any major expenses you see coming in the next twelve months, like a wedding, a move, or replacing that laptop that's held together with hope and duct tape.

Your budget is a living system that grows with you. Feed it regular attention, adjust when life throws curveballs, and it'll serve you far better than any rigid plan you abandon after two months.

As we wrap up this chapter, let's be real for a moment: if you're still reading, you're already ahead of most people your age. Why? Because you're taking action instead of just hoping your money situation magically improves. That matters more than you might think.

Here's what you now have in your financial toolkit: the 50/30/20 framework that gives you permission to actually enjoy your money while building wealth, digital tracking tools that show you where every dollar goes without the spreadsheet headaches, and strategies for handling variable income that smooth out those feast-or-famine cycles.

You've learned how to automate the boring stuff so your budget runs itself, and you understand why regular reviews keep your plan relevant as your life evolves. But the magic happens when you pick one strategy from this chapter – just one – and implement it this week.

Maybe it's setting up that automatic transfer to savings. Maybe it's finally linking your accounts to a tracking app. Maybe it's calculating your baseline income if you're freelancing. Start there. Build that habit. Then add another piece.

Think of it like working out – you don't walk into the gym and immediately bench press 200 pounds. You start with what you can handle, stay consistent, and gradually increase the weight. Your financial fitness works exactly the same way.

Remember that your budget should feel like freedom, not a financial straitjacket. If you're constantly stressed about every coffee purchase or feeling guilty about spending money on things you genuinely enjoy, something's wrong with your system – not with you. The goal is creating a money management framework that supports both your Netflix-and-takeout nights and your long-term dreams of financial security.

One final thought before we move on: every dollar you intentionally direct toward your goals – whether that's $5 or $500 – is a vote for the future you're building. Those votes add up faster than you think. In six months, you'll wish you had started today.

In the next chapter, we're tackling the elephant in the room for most us: debt. The budgeting skills you've learned here become your foundation for creating aggressive debt payoff strategies without sacrificing your entire quality of life. Because here's the reality – you can't budget your way out of high-interest debt without a solid plan, and you can't eliminate debt without the budgeting discipline to free up extra cash for payments.

Everything in personal finance builds on everything else. Master your budget now, and you'll have the clarity and control needed to demolish debt, build wealth, and design the life you actually want to live. That's not motivational fluff – that's just how this works.

Now stop reading and go automate one thing. Seriously. Your future self is waiting.

Chapter 4. Debt-Free Destiny: Conquering Student Loans and Credit Card Debt

The emotional and financial weight of debt affects more than just your bank account – it impacts your sleep, your relationships, and your ability to dream big. If you've ever felt that knot in your stomach when checking your credit card balance or avoided opening student loan statements, you're not alone. The average American in their twenties carries over $90,000 in total debt, a sobering reality that influences everything from daily coffee purchases to major life decisions like buying a home or starting a family.

Here's the truth that nobody tells you: people who are debt-free don't necessarily earn a six-figure salary, and they didn't the lottery. It's about understanding how debt actually works and developing a strategy that transforms what feels like an impossible mountain into a manageable path forward.

Whether you're staring down federal student loans, private education debt, credit card balances, or a combination of all three, this chapter will give you the tools to create your personalized roadmap to financial freedom.

Remember, the journey to becoming debt-free is a marathon, not a sprint. It requires patience, dedication, and a well-thought-out strategy. But with the right tools and mindset, you can break free and create the financial future you deserve.

Understanding Student Loan Types and Repayment Options

If you've ever stared at your student loan balance and felt your stomach drop, wondering how you'll ever pay it off, you're not alone. Student loans can feel like a weight you'll carry forever, but understanding exactly what you're dealing with is the first step toward freedom. Let's break down the types of loans you might have and the repayment options that can actually work for your life – not just in theory, but in practice.

Federal Loans: Your First Line of Defense

Federal student loans should always be your first choice when borrowing for education. Why? They come with protections that private loans simply don't offer – fixed interest rates, flexible repayment plans, and potential loan forgiveness. Think of them as the safety net you'll be grateful for when life throws you a curveball.

Here's what you need to know about the main types:

Direct Subsidized Loans are the golden ticket of student loans. If you qualified for these as an undergraduate based on financial need, the government actually pays your interest while you're in school and during grace periods. You can borrow up to $23,000 total, with annual limits ranging from $3,500 to $5,500 depending on your year in school.

Direct Unsubsidized Loans are available to both undergrads and grad students, regardless of financial need. The catch? Interest starts piling up from day one. Dependent undergrads can borrow up to $31,000 total, while graduate students can take out up to $20,500 annually, with a lifetime cap of $138,500 including undergraduate borrowing.

Direct PLUS Loans are for parents of dependent students or graduate students themselves. These require a credit check and carry higher interest rates – currently 8.94% for new loans in 2025-26, compared to 6.39% for undergraduate loans and 7.94% for graduate unsubsidized loans.

Choosing Your Repayment Strategy

Once you graduate, you'll face a crucial decision: which repayment plan fits your life? Federal loans offer several options, and picking the right one can save you thousands in interest or provide breathing room when money's tight.

The *Standard Repayment Plan* spreads your payments over ten years with fixed monthly amounts. It's the fastest way to become debt-free and minimizes total interest, but it also means higher monthly payments. If you can swing it financially, this is your best bet.

The *Graduated Repayment Plan* starts with lower payments that increase every two years over ten years. This works well if you're confident your income will rise steadily – think of it as a plan that grows with your career.

The *Extended Repayment Plan* stretches payments up to 25 years, dramatically lowering your monthly obligation. The downside? You'll pay significantly more interest over time. Use this option only if you truly need the lower payments to make ends meet.

Income-Driven Repayment (IDR) Plans tie your monthly payment to your income and family size, potentially reducing payments to as low as 10% of your discretionary income. These plans also offer loan forgiveness after 20-25 years of payments. Important heads-up: existing IDR plans are transitioning to a single Repayment Assistance Plan (RAP) by July 2028, so stay informed about changes that might affect you.

What About Private Loans?

Private student loans fill the gap when federal loans don't cover your full costs, but they come with significant trade-offs. Interest rates in 2025 range from 3.19% to 17.95% APR – a massive spread that depends on your credit score and whether you have a cosigner. The best rates go to borrowers with excellent credit, which most students don't have.

More importantly, private loans lack the flexible repayment options and safety nets of federal loans. No income-driven plans, limited deferment options, and no forgiveness programs. If you must borrow privately, exhaust your federal options first and shop around aggressively for the best rate.

Your Action Plan

Start by logging into your loan servicer's website and identifying exactly what types of loans you have. Make a simple spreadsheet listing each loan's balance, interest rate, and type. This clarity is power – you can't create a strategy without knowing what you're working with.

Next, evaluate your current financial situation honestly. Can you afford higher payments now to save on interest later, or do you need the flexibility of income-driven repayment? There's no shame in choosing a plan that fits your reality. You can always switch plans later as your situation improves.

Remember: your loan servicer works for you. If you're confused or struggling, call them. Ask questions. Explore your options. The worst financial decision is avoiding the problem and hoping it goes away.

The Debt Avalanche vs. Snowball Method: Choosing Your Strategy

Picture this: you've just organized all your debts into a neat spreadsheet, and now you're staring at the numbers wondering, "Where do I even start?" You've got that high-interest credit card at 22% APR, a smaller personal loan at 8%, and student loans hovering around 6%. Every financial guru seems to have a different opinion, and you're paralyzed by the choices. This is where understanding the debt avalanche and snowball methods becomes your secret weapon.

Here's the truth: both strategies work, but they work differently for different people. The avalanche method is your math-loving friend who always has the most efficient route mapped out. It tells you to attack your highest interest rate debt first – regardless of balance – while making minimum payments on everything else. So in our example, you'd throw every extra dollar at that 22% credit card, even if it has a $5,000 balance, while a $500 medical bill sits there waiting its turn.

Why does this make sense? Because interest is literally money disappearing from your pocket every single month. That 22% credit card is costing you far more than your 6% student loan, so mathematically, you'll pay less total interest and become debt-free faster by eliminating the expensive debt first. If you're the type who gets satisfaction from optimizing spreadsheets and knowing you're taking the most cost-efficient path, avalanche is calling your name.

Now let's talk about the snowball method, which is completely different. Instead of interest rates, you focus on balances – smallest to largest. You'd pay off that $500 medical bill first, then move to the next smallest balance, and so on. Yes, you'll likely pay more in total interest than with the avalanche method. But here's what the numbers don't capture: the psychological power of quick wins.

Research consistently shows that people who use the snowball method often stick with their plan because those early victories fuel motivation when the journey gets tough.

So how do you choose? Ask yourself these questions: Do you get more motivated by knowing you're saving the most money possible, even if progress feels slow? Choose avalanche. Do you need regular wins to stay committed, even if it costs a bit more in interest? Choose snowball. Are you somewhere in between? Consider a hybrid approach – knock out one small debt quickly for that initial win, then switch to avalanche for the rest.

Let's make this practical. Grab that debt spreadsheet you created and try this exercise. List your debts twice – once ranked by interest rate (highest to lowest) and once by balance (smallest to largest). Look at both lists. If your smallest debt also happens to have a high interest rate, both methods will point you in the same direction for your first target. If they're wildly different, think about your personality. Have you successfully completed long-term goals before, or do you tend to lose steam without regular encouragement?

Here's what matters most: pick one method and commit to it for at least six months. The worst strategy is constantly switching or, worse, making only minimum payments while you endlessly research the "perfect" plan.

Remember, both avalanche and snowball require the same foundation: making minimum payments on all debts while directing extra money toward your target debt. Both require consistency. Both lead to the same destination – freedom from debt. The path you choose simply depends on what will keep you moving forward when motivation wanes and life throws you curveballs. Choose the method that fits your brain, not just your budget.

Credit Card Debt Management: Interest Rates and Negotiation

Let me tell you something that might sting a little: that 24% APR on your credit card? That's a wealth-draining machine working against you every single day. While you're sleeping, eating breakfast, or scrolling through social media, interest is compounding on your balance, turning a $3,000 debt into something far more expensive if you're not strategic about attacking it.

Here's how credit card interest actually works, stripped of the confusing jargon. Your APR gets divided by 365 to create a daily periodic rate – so that 24% becomes roughly 0.06575% per day. Every morning, the card company calculates interest on your average daily balance, and if you're carrying a balance month to month, that interest compounds.

A $3,000 balance at 24% APR costs you about $720 in interest annually if you only make minimum payments. That's $720 that could have gone toward your emergency fund, retirement account, or that trip you've been dreaming about.

The good news? You have more power than you think. Most credit cards offer a grace period – typically 21-25 days after your statement closes – where new purchases don't accrue interest *if* you pay your full statement balance by the due date. This is your golden ticket. Pay in full, and you essentially get a free short-term loan every month. But here's the catch: once you carry a balance, you lose that grace period on new purchases until you pay everything off and reestablish the pattern.

Your Interest-Slashing Game Plan

Start by making payments more than once per month. Sounds simple, but it's powerful. If you can swing it, pay half your planned monthly payment mid-cycle and the other half before your due date. This reduces your average daily balance, which directly cuts the interest you're charged. Bonus: it also lowers your credit utilization ratio, potentially boosting your credit score.

Avoid cash advances like they're financial poison, because they basically are. Cash advances typically carry higher APRs (often 25-30%), have no grace period, and start accruing interest the moment you withdraw the money. That "convenient" $200 ATM withdrawal could cost you $50+ in fees and interest before you even realize it.

The Art of Negotiation: You Have Leverage

Here's something credit card companies don't advertise: they'd rather keep you as a customer than lose you to a competitor. This gives you negotiating power, especially if you've been making on-time payments. I've seen countless people slash their APRs by 5-10 percentage points with a single phone call.

Try this script: *"Hi, I've been a customer for [X] years and always pay on time. I've received offers from other cards with lower rates. Can you review my account and lower my APR?"*

Be polite but direct. If the first representative can't help, ask to speak with the retention department – they have more authority to make deals.

If you're genuinely struggling, ask about hardship programs. Many issuers offer temporary reduced rates, waived fees, or structured payment plans for customers experiencing financial difficulties. The key word is *temporary* – usually 6-12 months – but that breathing room can make the difference between staying afloat and drowning in debt.

Balance Transfers: Proceed with Caution

Those 0% balance transfer offers flooding your mailbox can be tempting, and sometimes they make sense. But read the fine print obsessively. Most charge a 3-5% transfer fee upfront, and if you don't pay off the entire balance before the promotional period ends (typically 12-18 months), you'll face retroactive interest at a potentially higher rate. Only pursue this if you have a realistic plan to eliminate the debt during the promo period.

Document everything. When you negotiate a lower rate or payment plan, get the terms in writing via email or letter. Set up automatic payments aligned to your new agreement to avoid accidentally reverting to old terms or triggering late fees.

Remember: credit card companies are businesses, not charities, but they're also motivated to keep you as a customer. Come to negotiations confidently, armed with knowledge about your payment history and competitive offers. You'd be surprised how often a simple ask transforms your financial situation.

Creating a Debt Payoff Timeline and Tracking Progress

Here's the moment of truth: you know your debt numbers, you've picked your payoff method, and now you need a concrete plan with actual dates on a calendar. Without a timeline, debt payoff feels like wandering through fog – you're moving, but you have no idea how far you've come or when you'll finally arrive. Let's build you a roadmap with real milestones you can see, track, and celebrate.

Start by gathering the essentials for every single debt you owe: current balance, interest rate (APR), minimum monthly payment, and debt type. I know, it's tedious. Do it anyway. Grab your latest statements or log into your accounts right now. Create a simple spreadsheet or use a notes app – whatever works for your brain. This information is the foundation of everything that follows, and guessing will sabotage your timeline before you even start.

Next, figure out your total monthly debt payoff budget. Add up all your minimum payments, then ask yourself honestly: how much extra can I consistently throw at debt each month? Notice I said *consistently*, not "I'll pay $500 extra this month when I'm motivated and $50 next month when I'm tired." Pick a realistic number you can maintain even during tough weeks. Maybe it's $100. Maybe it's $300. There's no judgment here, only math and commitment.

Now comes the satisfying part: plug your numbers into a debt payoff calculator. Bankrate's calculator lets you enter up to 10 debts and generates a customized schedule showing exactly which debt to target and when each will be eliminated. Credit Karma's tool is fantastic for running "what if" scenarios – you can see how adding just $50 or $100 more per month dramatically shortens your timeline and slashes total interest. For example, paying $1,000 monthly on a $10,000 credit card balance at 21.56% APR gets you debt-free in roughly 12 months with about $1,206 in interest. Drop that payment to $500 monthly? You're looking at 26 months and approximately $2,605 in interest. That's a 14-month difference and $1,400 saved just by doubling your payment.

Once your calculator spits out your timeline, translate those projections into calendar dates. Write them down: "Credit Card A paid off by June 2026. Student Loan 1 zeroed by March 2027. Completely debt-free by November 2028." Put these dates somewhere you'll see them – your phone's lock screen, a sticky note on your bathroom mirror, wherever works. These aren't just numbers; they're promises you're making to your future self.

Your Monthly Tracking Ritual

Set a recurring calendar reminder for the same day each month – maybe the day after payday. Spend 15 minutes updating your tracking system with current balances, payments made, and interest charged. Compare your actual balance to what your calculator predicted. Are you ahead of schedule? Behind? Exactly on track? This monthly check-in keeps you honest and lets you catch problems early.

Create a one-page dashboard that shows your debts ranked by your chosen method, this month's payments, remaining balances, and your next milestone date. Keep it simple – you want something you can glance at in 30 seconds and immediately know where you stand.

Quarterly Reality Checks

Every three months, re-enter your updated balances into your calculator to refresh your payoff dates. Your APRs might change, your income might shift, or you might have made extra progress. Run new scenarios: what if you added another $75 per month? What if you put your tax refund toward debt? These quarterly reviews keep your plan aligned with reality and help you spot opportunities to accelerate.

Here's a critical trap to avoid: as your balances shrink, minimum payments often decrease. Don't let your total monthly payment drop. If you were paying $800 total across all debts, keep paying $800 even as minimums fall. This maintains your momentum and prevents "payment erosion" that keeps you in debt longer.

When unexpected expenses hit – and they will – tap your emergency fund rather than adding new debt. Then temporarily reduce to minimum payments until you recover, and jump back into your aggressive strategy as soon as possible.

Avoiding Debt Traps and Predatory Lending

Let's talk about something that might make you uncomfortable: those "easy money" offers that pop up when you're desperate. You know the ones – payday loans promising cash in minutes, private student loan companies guaranteeing approval regardless of credit, or for-profit schools assuring you that their expensive program will land you a six-figure job.

These aren't opportunities. They're traps designed to extract money from people who can least afford it.

Here's what predatory lending actually looks like in your daily life. You're scrolling through your phone, stressed about rent, and an ad appears: "Get $500 by tomorrow! Bad credit OK!" The application takes five minutes, and suddenly money appears in your account.

What they don't emphasize is the 400% APR that turns your $500 loan into $700 in just a few months. Or the automatic rollovers that keep you paying fees indefinitely without touching the principal.

This is the debt trap – a cycle where you're perpetually paying without ever getting free.

Student loans present their own predatory landscape, especially when for-profit institutions enter the picture. These schools have been documented targeting low-income students, maximizing federal aid extraction, and delivering credentials with minimal job market value. The result? Graduates drowning in debt with no realistic way to repay it.

Unlike credit card debt or mortgages, student loans are nearly impossible to discharge in bankruptcy – they literally follow you until death. This makes choosing your education financing carefully absolutely critical.

Red Flags You Cannot Ignore

Learn to spot predatory lending warning signs before you sign anything.

- Aggressive sales tactics and pressure to decide immediately are huge red flags.

- Legitimate lenders give you time to review terms and compare options.

- Promises of guaranteed job placement or specific income without verifiable data? Walk away.

- High upfront fees for loan applications, lack of transparent pricing, or terms buried in confusing legal language all signal danger.

- If a lender requires you to sign arbitration clauses that waive your legal rights, that's not standard practice – it's a trap door.

Your Protection Strategy

The hierarchy of safe borrowing is straightforward: federal student loans first, always. They provide standardized terms, access to income-driven repayment plans, deferment options, and potential forgiveness programs like Public Service Loan Forgiveness. Private loans should be your absolute last resort, and only after exhausting federal options completely.

Follow these concrete borrowing limits to avoid overextending yourself:

- Keep total student loan debt at or below your expected first-year salary in your chosen field.

- Maintain monthly loan payments at or under 10% of your projected gross monthly income.

- Run the numbers *before* you borrow, not after.

- Use the loan calculators at StudentAid.gov to project your actual monthly payments based on realistic salary expectations for your major.

- If you need a small-dollar loan, check with credit unions first – they offer products with transparent terms and reasonable rates, unlike predatory lenders.

When You Need Help

If you're already caught in a predatory lending situation, take action immediately. Nonprofit credit counseling services can review your situation and help you find solutions. Organizations like the National Foundation for Credit Counseling offer free or low-cost assistance. Legal aid clinics, particularly those focused on consumer protection, have successfully challenged predatory practices and secured relief for borrowers.

Check the National Student Loan Data System through StudentAid.gov before accepting any new loans. See exactly what you already owe and use repayment calculators to understand the total cost of additional borrowing. If a private lender or school is pressuring you to sign quickly, that pressure itself is your answer – say no and walk away.

Remember: legitimate opportunities don't require split-second decisions or prey on your desperation. Protect yourself by staying informed, asking questions, and never borrowing more than you can realistically repay based on verified salary data for your field. Your future self will thank you for the caution you exercise today.

Building Credit While Paying Down Debt

Here's something that might surprise you: paying down debt and building credit aren't opposing goals – they're actually partners in your financial transformation. I know it sounds counterintuitive. You're probably thinking, "How can I build credit when I'm drowning in payments?" But stick with me, because understanding this relationship is the key to unlocking better interest rates, rental approvals, and financial opportunities while you're still on your debt-free journey.

Let's start with what actually matters to your credit score. Payment history accounts for the biggest chunk – about 35% of your score. This means that simply staying current on all your accounts, even while aggressively paying down balances, protects and builds your credit.

The second major factor is credit utilization – how much of your available credit you're using – which makes up about 30% of your score. Here's where your debt payoff strategy directly improves your credit: every dollar you pay down on credit cards lowers your utilization ratio, which can boost your score within weeks.

Think about it this way: if you have a $5,000 credit limit and you're carrying a $4,000 balance, you're using 80% of your available credit. That's hurting your score. Pay that balance down to $1,500, and suddenly you're at 30% utilization – a threshold that credit scoring models favor. You're simultaneously reducing debt *and* improving your credit profile.

Your Dual-Purpose Action Plan

First, automate minimum payments on every single account. Set these up today, not tomorrow. Missing even one payment can tank your score by 100 points and stay on your report for seven years. Automation removes the risk of human error when life gets hectic.

Second, focus your extra payments on credit cards rather than installment loans like student debt. Why? Because paying down revolving credit (cards) improves your utilization ratio and impacts your score faster.

According to Experian, "As a general rule, prioritize past-due accounts and high-interest credit card debt over installment loans if you want to improve your credit." You're getting a double win – less interest paid and better credit scores.

Third, resist the urge to close paid-off credit cards. I know it feels satisfying to ceremonially cut up that card, but closing accounts reduces your total available credit and can actually increase your utilization ratio. Instead, keep the card open with a zero balance or put one small recurring charge on it (like a streaming subscription) and set up autopay to handle it. This maintains your credit history length and keeps that available credit working in your favor.

Strategic Tools That Accelerate Both Goals

If you're carrying high-interest credit card debt, a balance transfer card with 0% introductory APR can be a powerful tool – but only if you use it strategically. These promotions typically charge a 3-5% transfer fee but halt new interest for 12-21 months.

The key is creating a realistic payoff plan that eliminates the balance before the promotional period ends. Run the math: if you transfer $3,000 with a 3% fee ($90), you need to pay roughly $260 monthly to clear it in 12 months. Can you commit to that? If yes, you'll save hundreds in interest while your credit utilization drops and your score climbs.

Schedule a mid-cycle payment in addition to your regular monthly payment. Credit card companies typically report your balance to credit bureaus on your statement closing date. By making an extra payment before that date, you lower the reported balance and improve your utilization ratio – even if you're still carrying a balance month to month.

Track your progress monthly. Log into your credit monitoring app (most banks offer free access) and watch your utilization percentage drop as you pay down balances. Celebrate these wins. You're not just reducing debt – you're building the credit foundation that will help you qualify for better rates on your next car loan, apartment, or mortgage.

Remember: every on-time payment is a building block. Every dollar that reduces your credit card balance is doing double duty. You're not choosing between paying down debt and building credit – you're doing both, one strategic payment at a time.

The beauty of what you've learned here is that you get to customize it. Maybe the debt avalanche method resonates with your analytical side, and you're excited to save every possible dollar on interest. Or perhaps the snowball method speaks to your need for quick wins and psychological momentum. Both work. The "perfect" strategy is the one you'll actually stick with for the long haul.

Here's what I need you to do right now – not tomorrow, not next week, but today. Pull out that debt inventory you created. Look at those numbers honestly. Choose your repayment strategy based on your personality, not just the math. Set up automatic minimum payments on every account so you never risk a late payment tanking your credit score. Then calculate one realistic extra payment amount you can consistently direct toward your target debt. Even if it's just $50, that's $50 more than you were paying before.

Remember the key insights that will carry you through this journey: your payment history is building your credit with every on-time payment, so you're not choosing between debt freedom and creditworthiness – you're achieving both simultaneously. Your credit card balances dropping means your utilization ratio is improving, which boosts your score while reducing your debt.

Every negotiation with a creditor is worth attempting because you have more leverage than you think. And that emergency fund you're building alongside debt repayment? It's your insurance policy against sliding backward when life throws you curveballs.

The path ahead will test you. There will be months when progress feels painfully slow. You'll face unexpected expenses that force you to temporarily scale back your aggressive payments. You might watch friends take vacations or upgrade their apartments while you're channeling every extra dollar toward debt.

In those moments, come back to your "why." Why does financial freedom matter to you? What dreams are you protecting by eliminating this debt now?

Your debt-free journey is about reclaiming your choices. It's about building the financial management skills that will serve you for decades. It's about proving to yourself that you can set an ambitious goal and achieve it through consistent action.

In our next chapter, we'll explore investment strategies that transform you from debt eliminator to wealth builder. The discipline you're developing right now – tracking your progress, staying committed through challenges, making strategic financial decisions – will become the foundation for building lasting wealth. But first, you need to free up those resources currently going toward debt payments.

Your debt-free destiny starts with the next payment you make. Take what you've learned, trust your strategy, and take that first step. You've got this.

Chapter 5. Investment Strategy Guide: From Stocks to Crypto

The investment world can feel overwhelming when you're just starting out – endless options, confusing terminology, and the constant fear of making a costly mistake. But here's the truth: you don't need to be a financial genius or have thousands of dollars to start building wealth through investing. What you need is a clear understanding of the fundamentals and the confidence to take that first step.

Think about where you are right now. Maybe you've got some money sitting in a savings account earning barely any interest, or perhaps you've been scrolling through investment apps wondering where to even begin. You might have friends talking about cryptocurrency gains or coworkers discussing their 401(k) strategies, and you're feeling left behind. That uncertainty is completely normal – every successful investor started exactly where you are now.

The beauty of investing in 2026 is that the barriers to entry have practically disappeared. You can start with as little as $5, learn through user-friendly apps, and build a diversified portfolio without needing a finance degree. Whether you're drawn to traditional stock market investing or curious about digital assets like cryptocurrency, understanding your options is the first step toward making your money work as hard as you do.

Success in investing comes not from making perfect decisions, but from making informed ones and staying committed through market ups and downs. In this chapter, we'll break down everything you need to know about building your investment portfolio, from understanding stock market basics to exploring how cryptocurrency fits into a modern investment strategy. By the end, you'll have the knowledge and confidence to start your own investment journey, regardless of your starting point.

Understanding Stock Market Basics: From Individual Stocks to Index Funds

Here's what nobody tells you about the stock market: it's not actually complicated. What's complicated is cutting through all the jargon and fear to understand what you're really doing when you invest. Let me break it down in a way that actually makes sense.

When you buy a stock, you're buying a tiny piece of a real company. That's it. You become a part-owner, which means you get to share in the profits (through dividends) and potentially benefit when the company grows and other investors want to buy your shares at a higher price. The catch? If the company struggles, your investment can lose value too.

Think of it this way: imagine your favorite coffee shop decided to let customers become owners. You buy a share for $100. If the shop opens new locations and becomes wildly successful, other people might be willing to pay you $150 for your share. But if a competitor moves in next door and business tanks, you might only be able to sell it for $50. That's the stock market in a nutshell – you're betting on businesses you believe will succeed.

Now, here's where most beginners get stuck: should you buy individual stocks or invest in index funds? This decision matters more than you might think.

Individual stocks mean picking specific companies – maybe Apple, Tesla, or a smaller company you believe in. This can be exciting and potentially lucrative if you pick winners. But here's the reality: even professional investors struggle to consistently beat the market by picking individual stocks. You're competing against people who do this for a living, with teams of analysts and sophisticated tools. Plus, if you pick wrong, you could lose a significant chunk of your investment.

Index funds are the secret weapon most financial advisors won't emphasize because they're almost too simple. An index fund is a basket of stocks that tracks a market index like the S&P 500 (the 500 largest U.S. companies). When you buy one share of an S&P

500 index fund, you're instantly investing in Apple, Microsoft, Amazon, and 497 other companies simultaneously. One purchase, instant diversification.

Here's why index funds are perfect for beginners:

- You can't pick the wrong company because you own hundreds of them

- Fees are incredibly low, often under 0.1% annually

- No research required – you're betting on the entire economy, not individual businesses

- Historically reliable – the S&P 500 has averaged about 10% annual returns over the long term

- Set it and forget it – no need to constantly monitor or rebalance

Let me be honest with you: I started with individual stocks because it felt more exciting. I spent hours researching companies, reading financial statements, and convincing myself I could outsmart the market. After a year of stress and mediocre returns, I moved most of my portfolio into index funds. My returns improved, my stress disappeared, and I got my evenings back.

Getting started is simpler than you think. You'll need a brokerage account, which you can open online in about ten minutes with companies like Fidelity, Vanguard, or Charles Schwab. Many brokers now offer commission-free trading and fractional shares, meaning you can start investing with as little as $10.

One crucial thing to understand: the stock market operates on Eastern time, from 9:30 a.m. to 4:00 p.m. Some brokers offer after-hours trading, but liquidity is lower and price swings can be more dramatic – stick to regular hours when you're starting out.

The market is also forward-looking, which confuses many beginners. Stock prices don't just reflect how a company is doing today – they reflect what investors expect the company to do in the future. That's why a profitable company's stock might drop if investors expect slowing growth, or why an unprofitable startup's stock might soar on future potential.

My advice? Start with a broad-market index fund. Build that foundation. Once you've got a solid base and you've learned more about investing, you can experiment with individual stocks if you want. But honestly? Many millionaires built their wealth with nothing but index funds and patience.

Building a Diversified Portfolio: Asset Allocation Strategies

Here's what most investing advice gets wrong: it tells you to "diversify" without explaining what that actually means or why it matters to your life. Let me fix that right now.

Imagine putting all your money into a single tech stock – let's say it's the hottest company of 2026. You're convinced it's going to the moon. Then the CEO tweets something controversial, regulators announce an investigation, or a competitor launches a better product. Suddenly, your entire investment tanks 40% in a week. That sick feeling in your stomach? That's what diversification prevents.

Asset allocation is just a fancy term for not putting all your eggs in one basket. It means splitting your money between different types of investments – stocks, bonds, and cash – so that when one zigs, another might zag. The goal isn't to avoid losses completely (that's impossible), but to smooth out the ride so you can actually sleep at night.

Here's the framework I wish someone had given me when I started: think of your portfolio as having three buckets.

- **The growth bucket (stocks)** is where your money works hardest. Stocks are volatile – they'll swing up and down – but over decades, they've historically delivered the best returns. For someone in their 20s or 30s with time on their side, this should be your biggest bucket. We're talking 70-90% of your investment portfolio.

- **The stability bucket (bonds)** is your shock absorber. Bonds are basically loans you make to companies or governments that pay you interest. They're boring, and that's the point. When stocks crash, bonds usually hold steady or even go up. A new investor might allocate 10-25% here – enough to cushion falls without sacrificing too much growth.

- **The safety bucket (cash)** is your emergency fund and short-term savings. This isn't really part of your investment portfolio – it's your "life happens" fund sitting in a high-yield savings account. Keep 3-6 months of expenses here, separate from your investments.

Now, diversification goes deeper. Within your stock bucket, you need variety:

- U.S. and international stocks – don't just bet on America102 100

- Large companies and small companies – they perform differently in different conditions102 100

- Different sectors – tech, healthcare, energy, finance, consumer goods100 102

Trying to buy individual stocks in all these categories? That's exhausting and expensive. This is where index funds and ETFs become your best friends. A single total stock market index fund gives you ownership in thousands of companies instantly. One purchase, complete diversification.

Here's a simple starter allocation for someone in their late 20s with moderate risk tolerance:

- 70% Total U.S. Stock Market Index Fund

- 20% Total International Stock Market Index Fund

- 10% Total Bond Market Index Fund

That's it. Three funds, complete diversification, minimal effort.

But here's the thing nobody warns you about: your allocation will drift. Let's say stocks have a great year and suddenly they're 85% of your portfolio instead of 70%. You're now taking more risk than you planned. That's where **rebalancing** comes in – periodically selling some winners and buying more of the laggards to get back to your target percentages.

I rebalance once a year, usually in January. Some people do it when allocations drift more than 5% from target. Either works – just pick one and stick with it.

Your allocation should evolve as your life changes. Got a house down payment goal in three years? Move some money toward bonds and cash. Married with dual incomes and a stable emergency fund? Maybe you can handle more stocks. The allocation that's right for you depends on your timeline, your stomach for volatility, and your financial cushion.

The biggest mistake I see? People create a perfect allocation and then panic-sell during the first market drop, destroying the whole strategy. Diversification only works if you stick with it through the inevitable downturns. That's why starting with an allocation you can emotionally handle matters more than finding the "optimal" one.

Start simple, stay consistent, and adjust as your life evolves. That's the real secret to building wealth through diversification.

Risk Management: Understanding and Managing Investment Risk

Let's talk about the thing that keeps most people from investing: fear. Not fear of losing everything – though that's part of it – but fear of making the wrong move, of being that person who bought high and sold low, of watching your hard-earned money evaporate because you didn't understand what you were doing.

Here's what I learned the hard way: you can't eliminate risk entirely, but you can manage it. And once you understand how, investing becomes a lot less scary.

What Risk Actually Means (And Why It's Not All Bad)

When financial experts talk about "risk," they're really talking about uncertainty – the chance that your investment won't perform exactly as you hoped. Sometimes that means losing money. But sometimes it means earning less than expected, or having your investment's value swing wildly even though it ends up fine in the long run.

Here's the part nobody emphasizes enough: different investments carry different types of risk. Stocks? They're volatile – they'll bounce around, sometimes dramatically – but historically they've delivered the best long-term returns. Bonds? More stable day-to-day, but they face interest rate risk (when rates rise, bond prices fall) and inflation risk (your returns might not keep pace with rising costs). Even cash sitting in your savings account carries risk – the risk that inflation will slowly erode its purchasing power.

The key is matching your investments to your timeline and stomach for volatility. In your 20s and 30s, you've got time on your side. A market crash that would devastate someone retiring next year? For you, it's a temporary setback – maybe even a buying opportunity.

Your Risk Management Toolkit

Here's your practical checklist for managing investment risk:

Build your emergency fund first. Before you invest a single dollar, stash 3-6 months of expenses in a high-yield savings account. This prevents you from being forced to sell investments at the worst possible time – like during a market crash when you suddenly need car repairs.

Diversify broadly, then verify. Spread your money across different asset classes (stocks, bonds), geographies (U.S. and international), and company sizes. But here's the trap: owning five different funds doesn't guarantee diversification if they all hold the same top stocks. Check your fund holdings to avoid overlap.

Set an allocation and stick to it. For someone in their late 20s, a starting point might be 80% stocks and 20% bonds. Write it down.

This becomes your anchor when markets go crazy and your emotions start screaming at you to do something.

Rebalance annually. When stocks have a great year, they'll grow to become a bigger chunk of your portfolio than you planned – increasing your risk. Once a year, sell some winners and buy more of the laggards to get back to your target percentages. It feels weird, but it works.

Automate everything you can. Set up automatic monthly contributions. This removes emotion from the equation and helps you buy during both market highs and lows – a strategy called dollar-cost averaging that reduces timing risk.

Limit individual stock positions. If you want to invest in individual companies, keep each position to 5% or less of your portfolio. One company going bankrupt shouldn't wreck your financial future.

Place investments tax-smart. Put bonds and other tax-inefficient investments in your 401(k) or IRA. Keep stocks in your taxable account where long-term capital gains get preferential tax treatment.

Cryptocurrency Fundamentals: Digital Assets and Blockchain Technology

Let me be straight with you: cryptocurrency confuses the hell out of most people. You've probably heard friends bragging about their crypto gains, seen headlines about Bitcoin hitting new highs, and wondered if you're missing out on something huge. Or maybe you're just trying to figure out if this whole thing is legitimate or just internet money that'll disappear tomorrow.

Here's what you actually need to know.

Cryptocurrency is digital money that exists entirely online, secured by complex math (cryptography) instead of banks or governments. When you send crypto to someone, there's no bank processing the transaction – it happens directly between you and them through a network of computers around the world. That's the "peer-to-peer" part everyone talks about.

The technology making this possible is called blockchain. Think of it as a digital record book that thousands of people have copies of. Every time someone makes a transaction, it gets recorded on a new "page" (called a block) that links to the previous page. Once something's written, it can't be erased or changed – everyone's copy would show the tampering. This creates a permanent, transparent record that no single person or company controls.

Here's why that matters: traditional money requires you to trust banks, payment processors, and governments to handle your transactions correctly. Cryptocurrency removes that middleman. The network itself – through this blockchain system – verifies everything is legitimate.

The Different Types of Digital Assets

Not all crypto is the same. Bitcoin was the first and remains the most well-known – it's basically digital gold, designed to be a store of value. Then you've got thousands of other cryptocurrencies (called "altcoins"), each with different purposes. Some, like Ethereum, let developers build applications on top of them. Others focus on faster transactions or more privacy.

You'll also hear about things like NFTs (non-fungible tokens) – unique digital items like art or collectibles that prove ownership through blockchain. Whether these have lasting value is still being figured out, honestly.

Should You Actually Invest in Crypto?

Here's my take after watching friends make and lose money in this space: cryptocurrency is speculative. It's not like buying a share of Apple, where you own part of a profitable company. Crypto's value comes entirely from what other people are willing to pay for it. That makes it volatile as hell.

I've seen Bitcoin drop 50% in a matter of weeks, then recover and hit new highs months later. If that kind of swing would keep you up at night or make you panic-sell, crypto probably isn't for you – at least not yet.

If you do decide to invest, follow these rules:

Start tiny. Put in only what you can genuinely afford to lose completely. I'm talking 5% of your investment portfolio max – maybe less when you're starting out.

Stick to the big names. Bitcoin and Ethereum have been around longest and have the most real-world adoption. Random coins promising to "moon" are usually garbage.

Use reputable exchanges. Coinbase, Kraken, and Gemini are established platforms with decent security. Avoid sketchy websites promising guaranteed returns – those are scams.

Understand it's not reversible. Send crypto to the wrong address? It's gone forever. There's no customer service number to call. This isn't like disputing a credit card charge.

Don't try to time it. If you're investing in crypto, treat it like a long-term bet on the technology, not a get-rich-quick scheme. Dollar-cost averaging – investing small amounts regularly – helps smooth out the insane volatility.

Investment Platforms and Tools: Choosing the Right Investment Vehicles

Choosing the right investment platform is crucial for your financial journey – it's like picking the right tool for a job. With numerous options available, from traditional brokers to modern mobile apps, understanding which platform aligns with your goals and experience level can make the difference between a smooth investing experience and unnecessary frustration.

When evaluating investment platforms, there are three primary categories: full-service brokers for beginners, mobile-first/low-cost brokers, and robo-advisors. Each serves different needs and offers unique advantages for new investors starting their investment journey.

Full-service brokers like Fidelity and Charles Schwab offer comprehensive educational resources, intuitive user interfaces, and robust planning tools. These platforms typically provide access to a wide range of investment vehicles, including stocks, bonds, ETFs, and mutual funds. Fidelity, for instance, stands out with its "Stocks by the Slice" program, allowing investors to purchase fractional shares and build diversified portfolios with small amounts of money.

Here are key features to prioritize when choosing an investment platform:

Fractional share investing capabilities to enable diversification with small budgets1

- Strong educational resources and goal planning tools

- Paper trading options to practice without risking real money

- Low or transparent fee structures

- Responsive customer support and built-in safety features

- Automation capabilities for recurring investments

For those seeking a more hands-off approach, robo-advisors like Betterment, Schwab Intelligent Portfolios, and Wealthfront offer automated portfolio management aligned with your risk tolerance and time horizon. These platforms handle the heavy lifting of investment selection and rebalancing, making them ideal for investors who prefer a set-and-forget situation.

Mobile-first platforms like Robinhood and SoFi Active Investing have revolutionized the investment landscape with commission-free trading and user-friendly interfaces. While these platforms make investing more accessible, it's important to note that their streamlined philosophy might not provide the comprehensive educational resources found in full-service brokers.

When starting your investment journey, look into something simple and structured. Begin with a low-fee broker that offers fractional shares and strong educational resources. Set up automatic transfers and recurring purchases of broad-market ETFs or a target allocation. This approach helps build good investing habits while minimizing the risk of making emotional decisions during market volatility.

Risk management features should be a key consideration in your platform selection. Look for tools that enable dollar-cost averaging, provide diversification options through low-cost index ETFs, and include safety features that help prevent costly mistakes. Many platforms now offer warnings and restrictions on complex trades, which can be particularly valuable for newer investors.

If you're feeling overwhelmed by the selection process, think about this simplified decision framework:

Choose a robo-advisor if you want the simplest path to a diversified portfolio with minimal time investment115

Select a full-service broker like Fidelity or Schwab if you value education and want more control over your investments114 117

Opt for a mobile-first platform if you prioritize ease of use and want access to features like cryptocurrency trading115 117

Remember that you can always switch or use multiple platforms as your needs and expertise evolve. The most important factor is selecting a platform that makes you comfortable enough to start investing and stick with your long-term financial goals.

As you evaluate different platforms, pay special attention to the fee structures. While many brokers now offer commission-free trading for stocks and ETFs, other fees might apply, such as account maintenance fees or management fees for robo-advisors. Understanding these costs upfront helps ensure they don't eat into your investment returns over time.

Ultimately, the best investment platform for you is one that aligns with your goals, provides the tools you need to succeed, and makes you feel confident in your investment decisions.

Long-term Investment Strategies: Goal-Based Portfolio Management

Here's what most people get wrong about long-term investing: they think it's about picking the perfect stocks or timing the market just right. But the real secret? It's about matching your investments to your actual life goals, and then having the discipline to stick with the plan when things get messy.

I learned this the hard way. When I first started investing, I threw money at whatever seemed hot without thinking about *why* I was investing or *when* I'd need the money. A few market dips later, I was panic-checking my portfolio daily and second-guessing every decision. Sound familiar?

Goal-based portfolio management changed everything for me. Instead of chasing returns, I started building separate investment strategies for different goals, each with its own timeline and risk level. Suddenly, investing made sense.

Match Your Money to Your Timeline

Think about your goals right now. Maybe you're saving for a house down payment in five years, building your retirement fund for forty years from now, and planning a big trip in two years. Here's the thing: these goals need completely different plans of attack.

Short-term goals (0-3 years) can't handle market volatility. If you need that money for a wedding or car down payment next year, keep it in a high-yield savings account or money market fund. Yes, the returns are lower, but you won't be forced to sell investments at a loss when the market inevitably dips right before you need the cash.

Intermediate goals (3-10 years) can handle some risk. For that house down payment in five years, look into something more balanced – maybe 50-60% in stock index funds and the rest in bonds. You get growth potential while limiting downside risk as your goal date approaches.

Long-term goals (10+ years) are where you can really harness the power of compounding. For retirement, new investors can typically handle 80-90% stocks, gradually shifting to more conservative allocations as retirement nears. Time is your biggest advantage here, because you can ride out market storms and benefit from long-term growth.

Build Your Goal-Based Investment Map

Here's a simple framework I use. Write down each major financial goal, then assign it to the right bucket:

- Emergency fund (immediate access): High-yield savings, 3-6 months of expenses

- Down payment fund (5-7 years): 60% total stock market index / 40% bond index; shift to 40/60 stocks/bonds by year four

- Retirement (35+ years): Start with 90% global stocks / 10% bonds in your 401(k) and Roth IRA; reduce equity allocation gradually after age 45

Use the Right Accounts for Each Goal

This is where most people leave money on the table. For retirement goals, prioritize accounts in this order: capture your full employer 401(k) match first, then max out a Roth IRA, then go back to additional 401(k) contributions. The tax advantages compound dramatically over decades.

For intermediate goals like a house down payment, use a taxable brokerage account. You'll have flexibility to withdraw without penalties, and if you hold investments for over a year, you'll benefit from lower long-term capital gains tax rates.

Keep It Simple and Automatic

The best investment strategy is one you'll actually stick with. I automate everything – contributions go out the day after payday, before I can spend the money elsewhere. My retirement accounts get their allocation, my house fund gets its contribution, and I don't have to think about it.

For most goals, broad-market index funds are your best friend. A total U.S. stock market fund and a total international fund give you instant diversification at rock-bottom fees (often under 0.10%). Simple, effective, and proven.

Rebalance and Adjust

Once a year, check whether your allocations have drifted. If stocks had a great year, they might now represent 70% of your intermediate-goal portfolio instead of your target 60%. Sell some winners, buy more bonds, and get back on track.

As life changes – career shifts, marriage, kids – revisit your goals and adjust accordingly. Goal-based investing isn't set-and-forget; it's set-and-review-annually.

The peace of mind this brings? That's the real return. You'll stop obsessing over daily market moves because you know each dollar has a purpose and a timeline. That confidence lets you stay invested through the inevitable downturns, and that's how wealth actually gets built.

Let's be real about what we've covered here. You've learned that successful investing isn't about picking the next hot stock or timing the market perfectly. It's about understanding the fundamentals – knowing the difference between individual stocks and index funds, grasping why diversification actually protects your money, and recognizing that risk management helps you build a portfolio you can stick with through inevitable market storms.

You've also learned that the investment landscape in 2026 offers unprecedented accessibility. You can start with $5, build a diversified portfolio through fractional shares, and access the same investment vehicles that millionaires use, all from your phone. The barriers that kept previous generations from investing early? They're basically gone. What matters now is knowledge and action.

Here's what I want you to do next. Don't try to implement everything at once. Start with one concrete step this week. Maybe it's opening a brokerage account, maybe it's setting up your first automatic investment of $25 into an index fund, or maybe it's just moving money from your checking account into a high-yield savings account while you continue learning. One action. That's it.

Remember these core principles as you move forward: invest regularly regardless of market conditions, keep costs low by favoring index funds, maintain proper diversification across asset classes, and stay focused on your long-term goals rather than daily market noise. These are proven strategies that have built wealth for millions of people who started exactly where you are now.

The next chapter will explore how to build multiple income streams through side hustles, adding another powerful dimension to your wealth-building strategy. But the investment knowledge you've gained here will make everything else more effective. When you're earning extra income from a side hustle, you'll know exactly how to invest those additional dollars for maximum long-term impact.

Your investment journey is uniquely yours. There will be market downturns that test your resolve and opportunities that tempt you to abandon your strategy. Stay committed to the fundamentals, keep learning, and remember that sustainable wealth building happens through consistent, informed decisions over time, not through perfect timing or lucky picks.

You've got the knowledge. You've got the tools. Now you just need to take that first step.

Chapter 6. Side Hustle Success: Building Multiple Income Streams

The rise of digital platforms and the accessibility of online marketplaces have created unprecedented opportunities for individuals to transform their passions into profitable ventures. Whether you're looking to supplement your income, explore entrepreneurial ambitions, or create a safety net of diverse revenue streams, the modern economy offers countless paths to financial growth.

Maybe you've felt it too – that nagging worry that one income source just isn't enough anymore. Rising rent, student loan payments, the cost of simply existing in 2026 – it all adds up faster than most paychecks can keep pace with. The good news? You already have skills, interests, and experiences that people will pay for. The challenge is figuring out how to package them, where to find your audience, and how to manage it all without burning out.

In this chapter, we'll explore proven strategies for identifying, launching, and scaling successful side hustles that align with your skills and schedule. You'll learn how to evaluate potential opportunities, manage your time effectively, and navigate the practical aspects of running a side business, from marketing and client management to financial organization and tax considerations.

Identifying Profitable Side Hustle Opportunities in the Digital Age

Here's the truth nobody tells you: the best side hustle opportunities aren't hiding in some secret corner of the internet. They're sitting right in front of you, disguised as problems people complain about every single day. The trick is learning to recognize them and understanding which ones are actually worth your time.

Let's start with what makes a side hustle genuinely profitable in 2026. You need three things working together: real market demand (not just what sounds cool), skills you either have or can learn quickly, and a business model that doesn't chain you to your desk 24/7. The most successful side hustlers I've seen focus on opportunities where businesses or customers have recurring needs – things they'll pay for month after month, not just once.

Take freelance digital marketing, for example. Every business with a website needs help with SEO, social media, email campaigns, or content creation. These aren't one-time projects; they're ongoing necessities.

You don't need a marketing degree to start. Many successful freelancers began by managing social media for a local coffee shop or writing blog posts for a friend's startup. The beauty of this path is that you can work remotely, set your own hours, and often secure retainer agreements that provide predictable monthly income.

E-commerce has evolved beyond the "get rich quick" schemes you might have seen advertised. The real opportunity lies in print-on-demand services and drop shipping models that eliminate the nightmare of inventory management. You can test twenty different t-shirt designs or phone case concepts without spending a dime on stock. When something sells, the product gets made and shipped.

Your job is finding the niche – maybe designs for veterinary students, or funny mugs for accountants – and driving traffic to your store. Start small, kill what doesn't work fast, and scale what does.

The creator economy deserves serious consideration, even though it requires patience. Building a YouTube channel, podcast, or newsletter won't pay your rent next month, but it can become a significant income source within a year.

Here's what surprised me: you don't need millions of followers. A podcast with just a few thousand engaged listeners in a specific niche – say, personal finance for nurses or productivity tips for grad students – can attract sponsors willing to pay hundreds or thousands per episode because that audience is exactly who they want to reach.

Online tutoring and coaching represent another high-potential category, especially if you can position yourself around high-stakes outcomes. General math tutoring? Competitive and low paying. SAT prep for students aiming at top universities? LSAT coaching for law school applicants? Career transition coaching for mid-level professionals? Now you're in territory where people pay premium rates because the stakes are high and the value is clear.

When you're evaluating potential opportunities, ask yourself these questions:

- Do people need this repeatedly, or just once?

- Can I deliver this service remotely and on my own schedule?

- What's my realistic path to the first paying customer within two weeks?

- Can this eventually make money while I sleep, or will I always be trading hours for dollars?

Here's your action plan:

- List three skills you have that others struggle with, even if they seem ordinary to you.

- Spend two hours researching what people in those areas charge on platforms like Upwork, Fiverr, or specialized marketplaces.

- Look at Facebook groups, Reddit communities, and LinkedIn posts where your target customers hang out. What are they complaining about? What problems keep coming up?

- Next, test fast and cheap.

- If you're thinking about freelance writing, reach out to ten small businesses in your area and offer a blog post at a discounted rate.

- If you're thinking about print-on-demand, launch ten designs this weekend and spend $50 on Facebook ads to see what gets clicks. You need real market feedback, not hypothetical planning.

Remember, the most profitable side hustle is the one you'll actually stick with long enough to get good at it. Start with something that leverages what you already know, provides value people will pay for today, and has room to grow beyond your personal time investment.

Time Management and Productivity Strategies for Side Business Success

Here's what nobody tells you about running a side business: you don't need more hours in the day. You need a system that protects the hours you have and directs them toward work that actually makes money.

Start by tracking your time for one full week. Write down everything – client work, emails, social media, administrative tasks. Be honest. You'll probably discover that you're spending hours on activities that generate zero income. Once you see where your time actually goes, you can make strategic decisions about where it should go.

The Eisenhower Matrix can be your decision-making lifeline. This simple tool sorts tasks into four categories: important and urgent (client deliverables with deadlines), important but not urgent (creating new templates, marketing), urgent but not important (most emails, minor admin tasks), and neither urgent nor important (scrolling social media, perfectionism). The magic happens when you schedule the important-but-not-urgent work before it becomes a crisis. That's where growth lives.

Here's the practical system that can transformed your schedule: implement time blocking with three protected weekly sessions. Monday evenings become your creation block – two hours for designing new templates or tackling custom projects. Wednesday nights are for sales and marketing – outreach, social media, updating your portfolio. Saturday mornings you handle operations – invoicing, emails, system improvements.

Treat these blocks like doctor's appointments. Non-negotiable. No "I'll just check this one thing."

Digital Marketing and Platform Selection for Maximum Reach

Here's what most people get wrong about marketing their side hustle: they try to be everywhere at once, spreading themselves so thin that they're invisible on every platform. The truth? You don't need to master every social media channel. You need to show up consistently where your customers actually spend their time.

Let's talk numbers that matter. Right now, 63% of Gen Z and 49% of millennials say social media ads or product reviews are the biggest influence on what they buy, which is way more than streaming ads or traditional marketing. If you're targeting people in their twenties and thirties (which you probably are), social platforms aren't just nice to have. They're where the money is.

But here's where it gets interesting: not all platforms work the same way. Instagram has about 2 billion users, with 60% under 35, and 61% of people use it specifically to discover products they want to buy. TikTok owns Gen Z's attention with short, punchy videos. Facebook? Still the king for older audiences and the number one platform where people actually complete purchases. YouTube builds trust through longer, educational content. LinkedIn connects you with professional clients for B2B services.

So how do you choose? Start with your customer. If you're selling trendy products to 18–25-year-olds, TikTok and Instagram Reels are your battleground. Targeting professionals who need your consulting services? LinkedIn and YouTube make more sense. Selling to a broader age range? Facebook's social shopping features convert browsers into buyers.

The platform matters, but your content strategy matters more. On TikTok and Instagram Reels, you've got about three seconds to hook someone before they scroll past. That means your first frame needs to stop thumbs mid-scroll to ask a provocative question, show a surprising transformation, or promise a specific solution. Save the setup and backstory for YouTube, where people expect depth.

Speaking of Instagram, 72% of Gen Z expects customer service through direct messages. If you start ignoring DMs or take days to respond, your sales will drop. But if you set up quick-reply templates and commit to responding within 24 hours, your conversion rate will jump. Your DMs aren't just messages – they're your storefront.

Social commerce is exploding, projected to hit $1.08 trillion by 2028. This means people don't just discover products on social media anymore. They buy them without ever leaving the app. Set up Instagram and Facebook Shops. Use product tags in your posts. If TikTok Shop is available in your market, test it. Make buying as frictionless as possible.

Here's your practical game plan: Pick two, maybe three platforms based on where your customers are. Don't spread yourself across six channels. Start with organic content – post 5-7 short videos per week on your primary platform, testing different hooks and formats. Track what gets saves, shares, and actual clicks to your offer.

Once you identify your top-performing content (usually your best 10-20%), put small money behind it. Start with $10-30 per day boosting your winners. You're not trying to go viral. You're trying to get profitable attention from the right people.

One critical mistake to avoid: don't put all your eggs in one platform's basket. Algorithm changes happen. Features disappear. Build an email or SMS list from your social traffic so you own the relationship with your audience, not just rent it from Instagram or TikTok.

Test your first platform for 30 days. Post consistently, engage with comments, track what works. Then scale what's working and cut what isn't. You're not going to become a social media expert overnight.

The platforms will keep changing. Your ability to show up, provide value, and connect with real people? That's what builds a side hustle that lasts.

Financial Organization: Tracking Income and Managing Expenses

Let's be honest: the money part of running a side hustle is where most people either get serious or give up. You can have the best service in the world, but if you can't tell me how much you actually made last month – after expenses, after taxes, after everything – you're not running a business. You're just busy.

Here's your first move: separate your money. Open a dedicated checking account just for your side hustle income and expenses. I know it feels like overkill when you're just starting out, but trust me on this. Mixing personal and business finances is like trying to untangle Christmas lights in the dark – frustrating, time-consuming, and you'll probably break something. A separate account gives you instant clarity on what your side hustle actually makes and costs.

Next, set up automatic splits the moment money comes in. This is the "pay yourself first" principle applied to side hustle reality. When that client payment hits your account, immediately move percentages to different purposes: 25-30% to a tax savings account (high-yield savings works great for this), 20% to your emergency fund until you hit 3-6 months of expenses, and the rest you can allocate between business reinvestment and personal income. Automate these transfers so you're not relying on willpower or memory. The money moves before you can spend it.

Now, tracking expenses. Every. Single. One. Download a receipt-scanning app or just take photos with your phone and dump them in a dedicated folder. That $12 Canva subscription? Business expense. The mileage to meet a client? Business expense. The fancy coffee you bought while working at a café? Probably not, unless you're meeting a client – be honest with yourself here. At the end of each month, categorize everything: software and tools, marketing and advertising, supplies, professional development, travel and mileage.

Pick one day each month and do your "financial close." Reconcile your accounts, meaning verify every transaction matches your records. Review your category spending against what you budgeted.

Calculate your actual profit: total income minus total expenses. Export your bank statements and save them in a dated folder. This 30-minute habit prevents the year-end scramble and gives you real-time insight into whether your side hustle is actually profitable or just keeping you busy.

Track metrics that matter. Your savings rate – what percentage of total income you're actually saving each month. Your side hustle margin – income minus related expenses. How many months of expenses your emergency fund covers. These numbers tell you if you're building wealth or just spinning wheels.

The biggest mistake? Budgeting based on your best month. When you have a $3,000 month, it's tempting to think that's your new normal. It's not. Budget from your lowest predictable monthly income and treat anything above that as a bonus that goes straight to savings, taxes, or one-time investments. This keeps you stable when client work slows down or sales dip.

Financial organization isn't sexy. It won't get likes on Instagram. But it's the difference between a side hustle that builds wealth and one that just keeps you exhausted.

Legal and Tax Considerations for Multiple Income Streams

Okay, real talk: the tax and legal stuff is where most side hustlers either get their act together or end up with a mess that costs them way more than it should have. I know it's not exciting. Nobody dreams about filing quarterly estimated taxes or understanding self-employment obligations. But ignoring this part doesn't make it go away. It just makes it expensive and stressful later.

Here's what you need to understand: when you're self-employed, you're paying both the employee and employer portions of Social Security and Medicare taxes. That's self-employment (SE) tax, and it's 15.3% right off the top – 12.4% for Social Security and 2.9% for Medicare. Add your regular income tax on top of that, and you're looking at setting aside 25-35% of everything you make, depending on your tax bracket.

If you're running multiple side hustles – say, freelance writing and an Etsy shop – the IRS wants you to combine the net earnings from all your self-employed ventures when calculating SE tax. You can't treat them separately to reduce what you owe. Keep separate profit-and-loss records for each business so you know what's actually making money, but understand that tax-wise, they're all getting added together.

Now, let's talk about the difference between active and passive income, because it matters for taxes. Active income – your freelancing, consulting, rideshare driving – gets hit with both income tax and SE tax. Passive income, like certain rental properties where you're not actively involved, typically faces income tax but not SE tax. The IRS uses something called "material participation" tests to decide which is which, so keep detailed records of your time and involvement in each venture.

Here's your quarterly estimated tax reality: if you're making decent money from side hustles, you need to pay estimated taxes four times a year – April, June, September, and January. Miss these, and you'll face penalties on top of what you already owe. The easiest thing is to set up a separate savings account and automatically transfer 30% of every side hustle payment the moment it hits your account. Treat that money like it's already gone, because it is.

When clients pay you $600 or more in a year, they should send you a Form 1099-NEC. And if you hire contractors for your side business and pay them $600 or more, you'll need to issue them 1099s too. Get W-9 forms from anyone you hire at the start – don't scramble for tax information in January.

Business structure matters more than you think. Most people start as sole proprietors because it's simple – no paperwork, just report everything on Schedule C. But you're personally liable for everything that happens in your business. A single-member LLC gives you liability protection while keeping the same tax treatment. S corporations might save you on SE tax but require payroll compliance and more paperwork. Start simple, but revisit your structure as you grow.

Don't forget state and local obligations. Depending on where you live and what you're selling, you might need business licenses, sales tax permits, or local tax registrations. These vary wildly by location, so research your specific area or talk to a local CPA.

Track every business expense – software subscriptions, supplies, mileage, home office space if you qualify. These reduce your taxable income and therefore your tax bill. Keep receipts, take photos, use an app – whatever works, just document everything.

The 2026 tax year brings updated brackets and a standard deduction of $15,000 for single filers and $30,000 for married couples filing jointly. These inflation adjustments affect your estimated tax calculations, so don't just copy last year's numbers.

Bottom line: hire a CPA or tax professional once your side income hits $10,000-$15,000 annually, or sooner if you're confused. The few hundred dollars you spend will save you thousands in missed deductions and avoided penalties. Your side hustle should build wealth, not tax problems.

Scaling and Automation: Moving from Active to Passive Income

Here's the truth about "passive income": it's not really passive, at least not at first. But that doesn't mean it's not worth building. The real goal is creating income that isn't directly tied to your hours. You can earn while you sleep, while you're at your day job, or while you're actually living your life.

The shift from active to passive income follows a pattern. You start by doing everything yourself – taking orders, creating the work, handling customer service, managing the books. Then you systematically replace yourself in each area through automation, delegation, or by creating assets that sell repeatedly without your involvement.

Here's your roadmap for moving toward more passive income:

Start by documenting your current process for everything you do repeatedly. Write it down step-by-step, like you're teaching someone else. These become your Standard Operating Procedures (SOPs). Once you can see your process clearly, you can spot what to automate or delegate.

Identify which of your offerings can be productized. Can you turn your service into a template, course, or digital product that sells repeatedly? Custom designs can become template packs. A freelance writer might create content templates or a course on writing sales pages. A social media manager could sell scheduling templates and caption libraries.

Invest in the right automation tools. Email marketing platforms can nurture leads and sell products on autopilot. Course platforms deliver your content automatically when someone enrolls. Print-on-demand services handle production and shipping without you touching inventory. Start with one or two tools that eliminate your biggest time drains.

Then there is financial automation. Index funds and ETFs offer hands-off investment growth – set up automatic contributions and dividend reinvestment, and let compounding do the heavy lifting. This isn't a side hustle in the traditional sense, but it's income that grows without your active involvement.

Track your "time-to-revenue" ratio. If you're earning $1,000 but spending 50 hours to make it, that's $20/hour – still active income. If you're earning $800 from assets that need 5 hours of monthly upkeep, that's $160/hour – much closer to passive.

The goal is to gradually shift your income mix so more of it comes from assets, systems, and automation. Start with one product or one automated system. Perfect it. Then build the next one. That's how you move from trading time for money to building income that scales beyond your hours.

Look, I'm not going to sugarcoat this: building multiple income streams isn't some magic solution that happens overnight. But the digital economy in 2026 has created opportunities that simply didn't exist a decade ago. You can sell templates while you sleep. You can coach clients from your living room. You can build a content platform that generates income long after you hit publish.

The barriers to entry have never been lower, but that also means the competition has never been fiercer. What separates the side hustlers who build real wealth from those who just stay busy? Strategy, systems, and the willingness to pivot when something isn't working.

Here's your action plan for the next 30 days:

- Choose one side hustle opportunity based on a skill you already have and a problem people will pay to solve.

- Set up your financial tracking system – separate account, automatic tax savings, expense tracking.

- Block out three specific time slots per week for your side business and treat them like non-negotiable appointments.

- Pick one platform where your target customers spend time and commit to showing up consistently.

- And most importantly, track your time-to-revenue ratio so you know whether you're building a business or just staying busy.

Some months will be discouraging. Some clients will be difficult. Some ideas won't work. That's not failure – that's data. Use it to adjust and keep moving forward.

Financial freedom through multiple income streams is available to anyone willing to start small, learn fast, and build systems that work smarter instead of just working harder. Thousands of others are proving it right now. Your turn starts today.

Chapter 7. Your Wealth Creation Roadmap: Real Estate and Long-Term Planning

The journey to building substantial wealth often starts with a decision that feels both exciting and terrifying: buying your first home. In 2026, homeownership represents more than just having a place to call your own. It's one of the most powerful wealth-building tools available, offering both a place to live and an investment that typically appreciates over time.

I know what you're thinking: "Home prices are crazy right now, and I'm not sure I can afford it." You're not alone in feeling this way. Many of us look at the housing market and feel discouraged before they even start. But here's the truth: while homeownership requires planning and patience, it's more accessible than you might think, especially when you understand the strategies that make it work.

With proper research, planning, and patience, homeownership can be a powerful wealth-building tool, even when you're just starting out.

Why does homeownership matter so much for building wealth? Unlike rent payments that disappear each month, your mortgage payments build equity, so you're essentially paying yourself instead of a landlord. As property values typically increase over time, you benefit from appreciation while enjoying tax advantages that renters never see. In 2026, with innovative financing options and various first-time homebuyer programs available, getting started is more feasible than many you may realize.

This chapter will guide you through the entire homeownership journey, from understanding whether you're ready to buy, to navigating the financing process, to managing your property effectively. We'll explore how to evaluate neighborhoods and properties, secure favorable financing, and integrate homeownership into your broader wealth-building strategy. Whether you're thinking about buying within the next year or planning for a few years down the road, the insights here will help you achieve homeownership with confidence and clarity.

Remember, successful homeownership is about creating a comprehensive plan that aligns with your financial goals and lifestyle. Thorough market research, starting with what you can afford, and viewing your home as both a place to live and a long-term investment. Let's dive into how you can make homeownership work for your wealth-building journey.

Real Estate Investment Fundamentals: Types of Properties and Investment Strategies

Understanding the fundamentals of real estate starts with recognizing one simple truth: your home can be both a place to live *and* a powerful wealth-building asset. While investment properties and rental income strategies exist, the most accessible and impactful real estate decision most of us will make is buying their first home. This single choice can set the foundation for long-term financial security in ways that renting simply cannot match.

When you pay rent each month, that money is gone forever, and it builds wealth for your landlord, not for you. But when you own your home, every mortgage payment builds equity, essentially paying your future self. According to research on wealth accumulation, homeownership remains one of the most reliable paths to building net worth over time. Your home appreciates as property values increase, you benefit from valuable tax deductions on mortgage interest, and you gain the stability of fixed housing costs while rents around you continue climbing.

Think about what happens over a typical thirty-year mortgage. Let's say you buy a home for $250,000 with a 20% down payment. Your monthly mortgage payment stays relatively stable (aside from property tax and insurance adjustments), but two powerful forces work in your favor simultaneously. First, you're gradually paying down the loan principal, building equity with each payment. Second, if your home appreciates at just 3% annually – a conservative estimate in many markets – that $250,000 property becomes worth over $600,000 in thirty years. Meanwhile, your neighbor who chose to rent has paid potentially double that amount with nothing to show for it.

The beauty of homeownership in 2026 is that you don't need perfect timing or a massive down payment to get started. First-time homebuyer programs exist specifically to help people like you enter the market. FHA loans require as little as 3.5% down, and some conventional loans now accept down payments as low as 3% for qualified buyers. VA loans offer zero-down options for eligible veterans and service members. These programs recognize that homeownership shouldn't be reserved only for those with substantial savings.

Location matters tremendously when buying your first home. You're not just choosing a property – you're choosing a neighborhood, a community, and a market trajectory. Research areas showing signs of growth: new businesses opening, infrastructure improvements, good schools, and reasonable commute times to employment centers. Properties in emerging neighborhoods often offer the best value, giving you appreciation potential while keeping your initial investment manageable.

The type of property you choose depends on your lifestyle and goals.

- Single-family homes offer privacy and typically appreciate well, though they require full responsibility for all maintenance.

- Condos and townhouses provide lower-maintenance living with shared amenities, perfect if you travel frequently or prefer a lock-and-leave lifestyle.

- Duplexes or small multifamily properties open the door to house hacking – living in one unit while renting another to offset your mortgage costs, though this requires embracing landlord responsibilities.

Before you start house hunting, get pre-approved for a mortgage. This process shows sellers you're a serious buyer and helps you understand exactly what you can afford. Lenders will evaluate your income, credit score, debt-to-income ratio, and employment history. A credit score above 620 opens most conventional loan options, while scores above 740 typically secure the best interest rates.

If your credit needs work, spend six months to a year improving it before applying – the difference in interest rates can save you tens of thousands over the life of your loan.

Remember that buying a home isn't just about the purchase price. Budget for closing costs (typically 2-5% of the purchase price), moving expenses, immediate repairs or updates, and ongoing maintenance. Financial experts recommend keeping 1-2% of your home's value in reserve annually for maintenance and unexpected repairs. A $250,000 home might need $2,500-$5,000 per year for upkeep, which is less than many people spend on rent increases, but still a reality to plan for.

Your first home probably won't be your forever home, and that's perfectly fine. View it as the first step in your wealth-building journey, like a foundation you can build on as your income grows and your goals evolve.

Market Analysis: Understanding Property Values and Growth Potential

Before you start searching for your first home, you need to understand what makes one neighborhood a smart investment and another a potential money pit. The difference between a property that builds wealth and one that drains your finances often comes down to understanding market fundamentals – and the good news is, you don't need a real estate degree to figure this out.

Think of market analysis like it's detective work. You're looking for clues that tell you whether a neighborhood is on the rise, holding steady, or heading downhill. In 2026, the national housing market is expected to see modest price growth of around 3% or less, which means choosing the *right* location matters more than ever. You can't just ride a wave of nationwide appreciation – you need to pick markets with real growth potential.

Start by looking at the big picture. Which cities and regions are people moving *to* rather than leaving? The Sun Belt continues to show strong momentum, with Dallas-Fort Worth leading the pack and several Florida markets making a comeback. But don't just follow the crowd – secondary markets like Raleigh offer compelling opportunities with better affordability and solid job growth. The key is finding places where people *want* to live and can *afford* to live.

Population and job growth are your first indicators. A city adding employers and residents creates natural demand for housing. Look for metropolitan areas with diverse industries – tech, healthcare, education, manufacturing – rather than cities dependent on a single employer or sector. When one company dominates a local economy, your property value becomes vulnerable to that company's fortunes.

Next, examine the supply side. How many homes are currently for sale in your target neighborhood? How long do they typically sit on the market? Rising inventory can shift formerly hot markets toward buyer-friendly conditions, giving you more negotiating power. But be cautious in areas with excessive new construction – elevated levels of new and speculative home inventory could limit price appreciation. You want a market with healthy demand but not oversupply.

Dig into the neighborhood itself. Visit at different times of day and days of the week. Are there good schools nearby? How's the commute to major employment centers? What about parks, grocery stores, and other amenities? These factors directly impact property values and your quality of life. A fifteen-minute difference in commute time or proximity to a highly rated school district can mean tens of thousands of dollars in property value.

Pay attention to infrastructure development. Is the city investing in new transit lines, road improvements, or community facilities? These projects signal growth and often boost nearby property values. Similarly, watch for new businesses opening – coffee shops, restaurants, and retail indicate confidence in the area's future.

Here's a practical tip: create a simple scorecard for favorite neighborhoods. Rate each area on job growth, school quality, commute times, inventory levels, and planned infrastructure improvements. This systematic comparison helps you move beyond gut feelings to data-driven decisions.

Don't overlook affordability metrics. Calculate the price-to-income ratio in your target market – how many years of median household income does it take to buy a median-priced home? Markets where homes cost less relative to local incomes tend to attract more buyers and show steadier appreciation. If you're stretching to afford the median home price, you might be better served looking at a more affordable nearby area with similar growth fundamentals.

One emerging factor: sustainability features. Homes with energy-efficient systems, solar panels, and smart technology are increasingly commanding premium prices, especially among younger buyers. Even if you're not initially focused on these features, neighborhoods where they're becoming common may see stronger long-term appreciation.

This year could offer opportunities to negotiate better deals in markets that were previously out of reach. The key is doing your homework, understanding local dynamics, and choosing a location with solid fundamentals that will support your home's value for years to come.

Financing Options: Mortgages, Down Payments, and Creative Funding

Once you've found a neighborhood with strong fundamentals and a property that fits your needs, the next question becomes: how do you actually pay for it?

For most of us, understanding financing options is where the dream of homeownership either becomes real or feels impossibly out of reach. The good news? In 2026, you have more paths to homeownership than you might think, and you definitely don't need a massive pile of cash sitting in your savings account to get started.

Let's talk about mortgages first, because this is probably the biggest loan you'll ever take out. A fixed-rate mortgage is the most straightforward option – your interest rate stays the same for the entire loan term, typically 15 or 30 years. This means your monthly principal and interest payment never changes, making it easy to budget. Most first-time buyers choose 30-year fixed mortgages because the longer term keeps monthly payments manageable, even though you'll pay more interest over time.

Adjustable-rate mortgages (ARMs) work differently. They offer a lower initial rate that's fixed for a set period – say, five years on a 5/1 ARM – then adjusts annually based on market conditions. ARMs can save you money if you plan to sell or refinance before the rate adjusts, but they carry risk. If rates rise significantly, your payment could jump higher than you can comfortably afford. For your first home, the predictability of a fixed-rate mortgage usually makes more sense.

Now, here's where things get interesting: you don't need 20% down to buy a home. That old rule? It's outdated. FHA loans require just 3.5% down, making them incredibly popular with first-time buyers.156 Conventional loans now accept as little as 3% down for qualified buyers.154 If you're a veteran or active-duty service member, VA loans offer zero-down financing with no mortgage insurance.157 USDA loans provide another zero-down option if you're buying in qualifying rural areas.

The catch with smaller down payments is mortgage insurance. Put down less than 20% on a conventional loan, and you'll pay private mortgage insurance (PMI) until you reach 20% equity – but you *can* cancel it eventually.154 FHA loans require mortgage insurance premiums (MIP) that often last the life of the loan.154 156 VA loans skip mortgage insurance entirely but charge a one-time funding fee.157 These insurance costs add to your monthly payment, but they also make homeownership accessible years earlier than saving 20% would allow.154

Don't overlook down payment assistance programs. Many states and local housing agencies offer grants or forgivable loans to help cover your down payment and closing costs. These programs typically target first-time buyers within certain income limits. Check your state housing finance agency's website – you might qualify for several thousand dollars in assistance that never needs to be repaid if you stay in the home for a specified period.

Beyond your down payment, budget for closing costs – typically 2-5% of the purchase price.154 These cover appraisal fees, title insurance, lender fees, and prepaid items like property taxes and homeowners insurance.154 Some sellers will agree to pay a portion of your closing costs as part of the negotiation, especially in buyer-friendly markets.

Here's a creative strategy that's gaining popularity: house hacking. Buy a duplex, triplex, or fourplex with an FHA loan (which allows up to four units with just 3.5% down), live in one unit, and rent out the others. Your tenants' rent payments help cover your mortgage, sometimes entirely. You're building equity while living nearly rent-free. It requires being a landlord, which isn't for everyone, but it's one of the fastest ways to build wealth through real estate in your twenties.

Before you start shopping, get pre-approved for a mortgage – not just pre-qualified.154 Pre-approval means a lender has verified your income, credit, and assets and committed to lending you a specific amount.154 This makes your offer stronger when competing with other buyers and helps you understand exactly what you can afford.

Remember: just because you're approved for a certain amount doesn't mean you should borrow that much. Leave breathing room in your budget for maintenance, repairs, and life's unexpected expenses. Your home should build wealth, not create financial stress. Choose a mortgage payment that lets you continue saving, investing, and enjoying your life – because homeownership is a marathon, not a sprint.

Property Management Essentials: From Tenant Selection to Maintenance

Here's something most first-time homebuyers don't realize until it's too late: owning a home means *managing* a home. The excitement of getting your keys can quickly turn to stress when your water heater fails at midnight or you're not sure how often you should be changing your HVAC filters.

But here's the good news – effective home management isn't complicated, and mastering these basics protects your investment while keeping your living space comfortable and safe.

Think of home management as preventive medicine for your property. Just like regular checkups keep you healthy and catch problems early, consistent home maintenance preserves your property's value and prevents small issues from becoming expensive disasters.

Property management experts agree: "The most cost-effective way to preserve residential properties is through proper management and preventive maintenance techniques." This isn't just about fixing things when they break – it's about stopping them from breaking in the first place.

Start by creating a home maintenance calendar.

- Your HVAC system needs servicing twice a year: once before summer cooling season and once before winter heating season.

- Change your air filters every 1-3 months depending on your system and whether you have pets.

- Clean your gutters twice yearly to prevent water damage.

- Test your smoke detectors and carbon monoxide alarms monthly and replace batteries annually.

- Schedule a professional plumbing inspection every two years to catch leaks before they cause major damage.

These routine tasks might seem tedious, but they're investments that pay real dividends. A well-maintained HVAC system lasts 15-20 years instead of failing at year 10. Clean gutters prevent thousands of dollars in foundation and roof damage. Early leak detection stops mold growth that could cost tens of thousands to remediate. When you're building wealth through homeownership, every dollar you save on emergency repairs is a dollar that stays in your equity.

Build relationships with reliable contractors *before* you need them in an emergency. Find a trusted plumber, electrician, HVAC technician, and handyman while you have time to research and compare. Ask neighbors for recommendations, read online reviews, and get quotes from multiple providers for non-emergency work. When that water heater does fail at midnight, you'll have someone to call instead of desperately choosing the first name that pops up in a Google search.

Keep detailed records of all maintenance and repairs. Create a simple spreadsheet or use a home maintenance app to log what was done, when, by whom, and how much it cost. Save receipts and warranties in one physical or digital folder. This documentation proves valuable when you eventually sell, showing potential buyers that the home has been well cared for. It also helps you track patterns and plan for future expenses.

Don't ignore small problems hoping they'll go away. That tiny roof leak, the toilet that runs occasionally, and the crack in your foundation are issues only get worse and more expensive over time. Address problems promptly when repairs are manageable and affordable rather than waiting until they become catastrophic.

If you've chosen the house-hacking route with a duplex or rental unit, tenant management adds another layer. Screen tenants carefully with consistent criteria applied fairly to all applicants. Use written lease agreements that clearly spell out responsibilities, payment terms, and house rules. Respond promptly to maintenance requests and document all communications. Good tenant relationships and proper property care protect your investment while generating the rental income that makes your mortgage more affordable.

Managing your home well isn't glamorous, but it's essential for building wealth through real estate. Every system you maintain, every small repair you handle promptly, and every dollar you save in your maintenance fund strengthens your financial foundation and protects the asset that's likely your largest investment.

Risk Management in Real Estate: Insurance, Legal Considerations, and Market Cycles

Let's talk about something most first-time homebuyers don't think about until something goes wrong: protecting your investment. You've saved for your down payment, navigated the mortgage process, and finally gotten those keys in your hand. Now what? Understanding how to protect your home from unexpected risks is essential for preserving the wealth you're building.

Here's the reality: homeownership comes with risks you never faced as a renter. When the roof leaked in your apartment, you called the landlord. Now *you're* the one responsible when things break, and they will break. But here's the good news – with the right preparation, you can handle these challenges without derailing your financial progress.

Insurance is your first line of defense, but not all policies are created equal. Many new homeowners make the mistake of choosing the cheapest policy without understanding what it actually covers. Your standard homeowners insurance typically covers damage from fire, wind, hail, and theft – but it might not cover flooding, earthquakes, or certain types of water damage. Read your policy carefully and ask questions. Does it cover the full replacement cost of your home, or just its current value? What about your belongings? What's your deductible?

These coverage gaps catch new homeowners off guard: mold damage, sewer backups, and home-based business equipment often require additional endorsements. If you're house-hacking with a rental unit, make sure your insurer knows – operating a rental without proper coverage can void your entire policy when you need it most. An umbrella liability policy adds extra protection beyond your standard coverage and typically costs just a few hundred dollars annually for substantial peace of mind.

Legal considerations might sound intimidating, but they're straightforward when you break them down. Before you close on any property, invest in a thorough title search to ensure there are no hidden liens or ownership disputes. It's worth the few hundred dollars to avoid discovering later that the previous owner's unpaid contractor has a claim on your property. If you're renting out part of your home, use a written lease agreement that clearly spells out everyone's responsibilities – verbal agreements lead to misunderstandings and potential legal headaches.

Keep detailed records of everything related to your home: purchase documents, inspection reports, receipts for repairs and improvements, insurance policies, and property tax statements. This documentation protects you legally, helps with tax deductions, and proves valuable when you eventually sell. Create a simple filing system – physical or digital – and maintain it from day one.

Understanding market cycles helps you make smarter decisions and avoid panic. Real estate markets move through predictable phases: expansion, peak, contraction, and recovery. In 2026, we're seeing a more balanced market after years of rapid appreciation, with modest price growth expected around 3% nationally. What does this mean for you? If you're buying now, you have more negotiating power than buyers had a few years ago. If you already own, don't stress about short-term value fluctuations – real estate builds wealth over decades, not months.

The key to navigating market cycles is staying focused on your long-term goals. Your home's value will fluctuate, but if you've bought in a solid neighborhood with good fundamentals – job growth, quality schools, reasonable commute times – you'll be fine over the long haul.164 162 Avoid the temptation to constantly check online home value estimates; they're often inaccurate and create unnecessary anxiety.

Integration with Overall Wealth Strategy: Balancing Real Estate with Other Investments

Real estate can be a powerful wealth-building tool, but its true potential emerges when strategically integrated into your broader financial portfolio. Understanding how to balance homeownership with other investments is crucial for building sustainable wealth while managing risk effectively. Let's explore how to create a harmonious blend that aligns with your financial goals without putting all your eggs in one basket.

Here's something many first-time homebuyers don't realize: your home is probably going to become your largest single asset, but that doesn't mean it should be your *only* asset. Think of your wealth-building strategy like a three-legged stool – you need multiple supports to stay balanced. Your home provides one leg through equity building and appreciation. Your retirement accounts (401(k), IRA) provide another through stock and bond investments. Your emergency fund and other liquid savings provide the third through financial flexibility and security.

The foundation of a well-balanced strategy starts with understanding the role your home plays in your overall net worth. According to research on household finance, while real estate often represents the largest component of household wealth, it's essential to avoid overconcentration in any single asset type. A diversified approach that includes stocks, bonds, and real estate helps protect your wealth while maximizing growth potential.

Here's a practical framework: aim to keep your housing costs (mortgage, taxes, insurance, maintenance) below 28% of your gross monthly income. This leaves breathing room to continue investing in your retirement accounts and maintaining your emergency fund.

Remember, your home builds wealth slowly through equity and appreciation, but your retirement accounts benefit from compound growth over decades. You need both working for you.

Liquidity management becomes crucial when you own a home. Beyond your standard emergency fund, maintain an additional reserve specifically for home-related expenses – think broken water heaters, roof repairs, or HVAC replacements. Industry standards suggest keeping one to two percent of your home's value set aside annually for maintenance and unexpected repairs. If you own a $250,000 home, that's $2,500 to $5,000 per year in a dedicated home maintenance fund.

As your career progresses and your income grows, resist the temptation to pour every extra dollar into your home through aggressive principal payments or expensive renovations. Instead, maintain balance. Continue maxing out tax-advantaged retirement accounts, which offer immediate tax benefits and long-term growth potential. Open a taxable brokerage account for additional investing once you've maxed out retirement contributions.

Your home equity is real wealth, but it's not liquid wealth. You can't easily tap it to cover an unexpected job loss or medical emergency without taking on debt through a home equity loan or line of credit. This is why maintaining diversified, liquid investments alongside homeownership is so important – they provide flexibility your home equity simply cannot.

Think about rebalancing your overall wealth strategy annually. As your home appreciates and you pay down your mortgage, real estate might grow to represent 40%, 50%, or even 60% of your net worth. When this happens, direct new savings toward your investment accounts rather than additional real estate to maintain diversification.

The Global Financial Crisis taught us valuable lessons about the importance of prudent leverage and diversification. Homeowners who had maintained emergency funds, continued investing in retirement accounts, and avoided overextending themselves weathered the storm far better than those who had concentrated all their wealth in real estate.

Your home should enhance your wealth-building journey, not dominate it. By maintaining balance, you create a resilient financial foundation that can weather market cycles and support your long-term goals.

As you move forward, remember these key principles:

- Start with thorough research and realistic expectations.
- Buy what you can comfortably afford, not the maximum you're approved for.
- Focus on solid neighborhoods with strong fundamentals.
- Maintain your property consistently.
- Keep your finances balanced and diversified.

Homeownership is within your reach. It won't happen overnight, and it requires planning and patience – but the wealth-building potential makes it worth the effort. Whether you're ready to start house hunting next month or you're planning for a few years down the road, the strategies in this chapter will guide you toward making informed decisions that align with your goals.

Your journey to building wealth through homeownership starts with a single step. Make sure it's a well-informed one.

Conclusion

You've made it! You've absorbed a lot of information, and I hope you're feeling energized rather than overwhelmed. Because here's the truth: everything you've just learned can change your life, starting today.

Think about where you were when you picked up this book. Maybe you were stressed about student loans, confused about investing, or simply tired of feeling like money controlled you instead of the other way around.

Now look at what you know. You understand how your mindset shapes your financial reality. You've got practical tools for budgeting that actually work with your lifestyle. You know how to tackle debt strategically, build investment portfolios, create additional income streams, and even plan for real estate investments.

That's powerful. But knowledge alone won't change anything. Action will.

I've seen too many people read books like this, feel inspired for a week, then slip back into old patterns. Don't let that be you. The only difference between people who achieve financial freedom and those who don't is consistent action on the fundamentals.

So here's what I want you to do right now, before you close this book: choose *one* thing. Not ten things. One. Maybe it's downloading a budgeting app and tracking your expenses for the next thirty days. Maybe it's setting up an automatic transfer of $50 to a savings account. Maybe it's finally opening that investment account you've been putting off. Whatever it is, do it today. Not tomorrow. Today.

Once that becomes habit, add another action. Then another. This is how you build momentum. Small wins compound into life-changing results.

Your starting point, your goals, your timeline are all uniquely yours. Maybe you're dealing with more debt than you'd like. Maybe you're earning less than you hoped. Maybe you're starting later than you planned. None of that matters as much as what you do next.

Financial freedom isn't about reaching some magical number in your bank account. It's about having choices. It's about not panicking when unexpected expenses arise. It's about pursuing opportunities because you want to, not because you desperately need the money. It's about building a life where money serves your dreams instead of limiting them.

You're going to make mistakes along the way. You'll overspend some months. You'll make investment decisions you later question. You might even face setbacks that feel devastating in the moment. That's all part of the process. What matters is that you keep learning, keep adjusting, and keep moving forward.

The financial landscape will continue evolving. New investment opportunities will emerge. Economic conditions will shift. Your life circumstances will change. Stay curious. Keep learning. Adapt your strategies as needed. The fundamentals we've covered will serve you well, but remain flexible in how you apply them.

Ten years from now, you'll look back on this moment as a turning point – but only if you act. Your future self is counting on the decisions you make today. So take that first step. Then take another. And another.

You've got this. Now go build the financial future you deserve.

Thank You for Reading!

I hope you found The Stress-Free Money Blueprint helpful and enjoyable!

Your feedback is invaluable to me and helps others discover this book.

If you could take a moment to leave a review,

I'd greatly appreciate it!

Patty

Visit the Cantelune Press website for more compassionate books that meet you where you are! https://cantelunepress.com/

Bibliography

References

Coambs, E. (2021, November 04). *4 Example Money Stories To Help You Understand Your Own*. Healthy Love and Money.

Hightower Advisors. (2023, November 28). *The Power of Your Money Story in Financial Planning*. Well-th Blog.

Samantha. (2019, August). *What's a money story? And how to find yours*. She Is Bold.

Clemons, L. (2023, May 16). *Money Stories and How They Shape Our Lives*. rtor.org.

Mayfield, A. (2025, April 28). *The Psychology of Spending: How Emotions Shape Our Financial Decisions*. EFL Global.

Cornerstone Private Asset Trust Company, LLC. (2025, March 12). *The Psychology of Spending*. Cornerstone Trust.

Redacción MAPFRE. (2023, December 18). *Emotional spending: what is it and how to manage it?*. MAPFRE.

Genesis Financial Group. (2024). *The Psychology of Spending: Understanding and Controlling Your Financial Behaviors*. Genesis Financial Group.psychology-of-spending-understanding-and-controlling-your-financial-behaviors

Spicer, T. (2024, April 16). *Book$mart: Top Financial Education Reads for Kids and Teens*. GreenPath Financial Wellness.

WECU. (2023). *Setting SMART Financial Goals*. WECU.

Desert Financial Credit Union. (2024, July 31). *Setting SMART Financial Goals*. Desert Financial.

Talbot, A. (2024, December 30). *Want to save money in the new year? Set S.M.A.R.T. financial goals*. Webster First Federal Credit Union.

SmartAsset. (2022, May). *SMART Financial Goal Examples.* SmartAsset.

OMB Bank. (2024). *How to Set SMART Financial Goals for 2025.* OMB Bank.

Langworthy, D. (2023, October 2). *Overcoming Money Blocks.* Fortress Financial Group.

Woodfield, T. (2025, July 22). *12 Big Money Blocks Even the Rich Have and How to Reverse Them.* Tiffany Woodfield.

Duffield-Thomas, Denise. (2023, August 15). *How to Clear Your Money Blocks.* DeniseDT.com.

Edwards, E.. (2020, April 1). *How Your Money Blocks Are Affecting Your Financial Confidence.* The Broke Generation.

Greer, A. (2023, February). *What Are Money Blocks?.* Ashlee Greer.

SmartAsset. (2024, July). *Values-Based Financial Planning: What It Is and How It Works.* SmartAsset.

Hill, T. J. (2023, March 02). *What To Know About Values-Based Financial Planning.* Asset-Map.

Willis, S. (2024, June 11). *What Is Values-Based Financial Planning?.* Asset Preservation Wealth & Tax.

AstuteWheel. (2021, May). *What is values based advice?.* AstuteWheel.

Roberts, M. (2023, August 05). *What is Values-Based Financial Planning and How is it Implemented at Syverson Strege?.* Syverson Strege.

Bank of Dudley. (2025, March 20). *4 Benefits of Online Banking.* Bank of Dudley.

Administrator. (2025, January 20). *20 Best Banking App Features to Stand Out in 2025.* Aress.

Inese & Alex & Linda & Santa. (2024). *7 Ultimate Digital Banking Trends 2025 to Elevate Financial Brands UX*. UXDA.

Bennett, R. (2025, April 29). *Digital banking trends in 2025*. Bankrate.

Kozielecki, P. (2023). *Must-Have Mobile Banking App Features in 2023*. Netguru.

Thompsett, L. (2024, November 26). *Digital Wallets Set to Revolutionise Global Finance by 2025*. FinTech Magazine.

Marqeta. (2025, April 23). *How digital wallets are transforming payments*. Marqeta.

Gong, J. (2025, May 22). *Top 7 Digital Wallet Apps to Know in 2025*. FreshBooks.

Hyman, V. (2024, December 12). *10 top payments trends for 2025 – and beyond*. Mastercard.

Market Pay. (2025, February 24). *Best Mobile Payment Apps: Which One Should You Choose?*. Market Pay.

Smith, G. (2025, January 07). *The Best Personal Finance Apps for Gen Z in 2025*. Made-in-China.com Business Insights.

Hannah H. (2025). *Top 10 Apps in 2025 for Building Financial Freedom*. Lithios Apps.

Vincent, E. (2025, July 16). *Seven of the Best Budgeting Apps for 2025*. Kiplinger.

NerdWallet. (2025, June 27). *Best Budget Apps of 2025*. NerdWallet.

Dieterich Bank. (2024, July). *Secure & Simple: Your Friendly Guide to Banking Cybersecurity*. Dieterich Bank.

Skinner, M. (2023, December). *Cybersecurity challenges digital banking*. HORNE.

Dimenna, J. (2025, April 29). *Gen Z and Millennial Banking Expectations: Customer Retention Strategies for Younger Generations*. Apiture.

Jasińska, D. (2024, December 18). *Cybersecurity in Banking: Threats and Mitigation Strategies*. Neontri.

Hyman, V. (2025, May 20). *How Gen Z is inspiring a reinvention of banking*. Mastercard.

CFI Team. (2023). *Automatic Bill Payment*. Corporate Finance Institute.

SmartAsset. (2025, January). *How to Set Up Automatic Bank Transfers*. SmartAsset.

Stripe. (2023, December 31). *What is an automated bill payment?*. Stripe Resources.

Paystand. (2024). *Automatic Bill Payment*. Paystand Blog.

SFCU. (2024, January 15). *Fraud prevention: Teens & young adults are 3X more likely to fall for scams*. SFCU.

First National Bank Minnesota. (2023, December 31). *Fraud Education*. First National Bank Minnesota.

Jeanne D'Arc Credit Union. (2024, February 12). *Get Scam Smart: How to Protect Your Money - Fraud Prevention Tips for Teens*. Jeanne D'Arc Credit Union.

TD Bank Group. (2024, February 28). *Young adults are prime targets for fraud on social media, but many are too embarrassed to admit they've been a victim of a scam: TD Survey*. TD Stories.

Finex Credit Union. (2022, July 21). *Avoiding Online Financial Scams in the Digital Age [Top 7 Safety Tips]*. Finex Credit Union.

NerdWallet. (2025, January 01). *50/30/20 Budget Calculator: How Much Should You Spend?*. NerdWallet.

Campbell, C. (2025, May 7). *What Is the 50/30/20 Budgeting Rule?*. Annuity.org.

John Hancock. (2019, April 11). *Budget 101: debunking the 50-20-30 rule*. John Hancock.

Citizens Bank. (2025). *What is the 50/30/20 budget rule?*. Citizens Bank Learning Center.

Mercieca, A. (2025, July 11). *The best business expense tracking apps and tools of 2025*. Ramp.

Emburse. (2024). *Top 8 Expense Management Mobile Apps for 2025*. Emburse.

Coast Central Credit Union. (2025, January 14). *Seven Steps for Budgeting with an Irregular Income*. Coast Central Credit Union.

Morrison, K. & Stueve, C. (2023, March 13). *Financial Wellness in the Gig Economy: Empowering Flexibility with Stability*. AFCPE.

M1 Finance LLC. (2025, January 31). *Budgeting for Freelancers: Effective Strategies for Variable Income*. M1.

Trailhead Credit Union. (2024, January 15). *How Portland's Gig Economy Workers Can Manage Their Finances*. Trailhead Credit Union.

Amegy Bank. (2024, July 26). *Tips for Budgeting With a Variable Income*. Amegy Bank.

Lainiotis, G. I. (2023, November 21). *Personal Finance for Teens and Young Adults: Financial Literacy Skills To Empower Your Future, Crush Your Debt & Build Smart Money Habits That Instill Lifelong Confidence*. Barnes & Noble.

Keane, R. (2024, October 12). *Financial Literacy for Teens Parents' Guide: Discover How to Teach Teenagers Smart Money Skills to Budget, Save, & Invest for a Secure Future*. Goodreads.

Keane, R. (2023, July 04). *Financial Literacy for Young Adults Simplified: Discover How to Manage, Save, and Invest Money to Build a Secure & Independent Future*. Goodreads.

Ferry, J. (2021, August 1). *Teen Guide to Financial Literacy*. Kirkus Reviews.

Smith, G. (2025, January 07). *10 Budgeting Hacks for Millennials in 2025*. Made-in-China.com Business Insights.

Crudu, V. & MoldStud Research Team. (2024, December 3). *Top Financial Planning Apps for Millennials - A Comprehensive Guide*. MoldStud.

Alleo. (2024). *How Millennials Can Master Budgeting and Long-Term Savings: 3 Proven Techniques*. Alleo.ai.

SuperAGI. (2025, July 1). *10 AI-Powered Budgeting Tools to Revolutionize Your Personal Finance in 2025: A Beginner's Guide*. SuperAGI.

Isler, N. (2025, April 28). *Top 5 Smart Budgeting Tips for Millennials*. Neil Isler.

Safier, R. (2025, January 27). *Types of Student Loans: Federal and Private [2025]*. Credible.

Howard, B. & Nam, J. (2025, July 29). *Federal vs. private student loans: What's the difference?*. Bankrate.

ELFI. (2025, May 30). *Understanding Federal Student Loan Rates for 2025-2026*. ELFI.com.

StudentChoice.org. (2025, June 20). *How to Compare Student Loan Offers in 2025 (And Avoid Costly Mistakes)*. StudentChoice.org.

EducationData.org. (2025, January). *Average Student Loan Interest Rate*. EducationData.org.

Wells Fargo. (2024, March). *Comparing the snowball and the avalanche methods of paying down debt*. Wells Fargo.

Yale, A. J. and Safane, J. (2025, April 30). *Debt snowball vs. debt avalanche: Which strategy is right for you?*. Business Insider.

Luthi, B. (2024, July 15). *Debt Snowball vs. Debt Avalanche Method*. Experian.

Fidelity Investments. (2025, February 25). *Debt snowball method vs. debt avalanche method: Which is right for you?*. Fidelity.

Munster, R. (2024, September 26). *Avoid Debt and Build a Strong Financial Future as a Young Adult*. Money Fit.

Sears, L. (2025, April 01). *Smart Strategies for Effective Debt Management*. WVU Extension.

The Yukon Project. (2024, January 15). *Debt Payoff Calculator - The Interactive Debt Calculator*. The Yukon Project.

Credit Karma. (2024, March). *Debt Repayment Calculator*. Credit Karma.

PocketGuard. (2023, August 11). *Debt payoff calculator*. PocketGuard.

Bankrate. (2025, April 04). *Debt Paydown Calculator*. Bankrate.com.

Financial Mentor. (2023). *Debt Snowball Calculator*. Financial Mentor.

Bodnar, J. (2010, August 30). *7 Strategies to Avoid the Student-Debt Trap*. Kiplinger.

Cornerstone Community Federal Credit Union. (2025, April 6). *Can Student Loans Become a Debt Trap?*. Cornerstone Community Federal Credit Union.

McArdle, E. (2013, July 01). *Debt Trap*. Harvard Law School.

Ferris State University. (2023, October 15). *Tips To Minimize Student Loan Debt*. Ferris State University Financial Aid.

Navy Federal Credit Union. (2025, February 26). *Debt Repayment Strategies*. Navy Federal Credit Union MakingCents.

DeNicola, L. (2025, January 16). *Which Debts Should I Pay Off First to Improve My Credit?*. Experian.

Equifax. (2023). *Strategies for Paying Off Debt*. Equifax.com.

Baird Wealth. (2025, April 10). *5 Strategies for Paying Off Credit Card Debt*. Baird Wealth.

Bank of America. (2025). *How to get out of credit card debt faster.* Better Money Habits.

Royal, J. (2025, April 23). *Stock market basics: 10 tips for beginners.* Bankrate.

NerdWallet. (2024, March 20). *Stock Market Basics: What Beginner Investors Should Know.* NerdWallet.

U.S. Securities and Exchange Commission. (2025, August 30). *Beginners' Guide to Asset Allocation, Diversification, and Rebalancing.* Investor.gov.

New York Life. (2024, April). *Asset allocation & diversification: a guide.* New York Life.

Vanguard Group. (2024). *Diversifying Your Portfolio.* Vanguard.

Vanguard Group. (2024, January 01). *Investment portfolios: Asset allocation models.* Vanguard.

FINRA. (2022, August 01). *Asset Allocation and Diversification.* Financial Industry Regulatory Authority.

Lin, Z. (2025, March 18). *3 strategies to help reduce risk.* Fidelity.

SoFi. (2024, February 26). *Investment Risk Management: Definition, Strategies & Examples.* SoFi Learn.

Cooke, J. (2025, March 24). *Best Investment Strategies for Young Adults: Building Wealth in Your 30s.* Cooke Wealth Management.

Brouillette D.. (2025, April 14). *Where to Start: Investing Basics for Young Adults.* DSB Rock Island Wealth Management.

Freeman Law. (2021, July). *Blockchain Technology Explained | What is Blockchain and How Does It Work?.* Freeman Law.

Susnjara, S. (2024). *What is blockchain?.* IBM Think.

Amazon Web Services. (2024). *What is Blockchain Technology?.* Amazon Web Services.

Coursera Staff. (2025, July 2). *Blockchain in Cryptocurrency: Beginner's Guide and Career Overview*. Coursera.

Botelho, I. (2024, July 03). *Blockchain Basics: A Simple Guide for Beginners*. Cardano Foundation.

Inskip, J. (2025, July 03). *Best Stock Trading Platforms for Beginners of 2025*. StockBrokers.com.

Royal, J. F. (2025, August). *Best online brokers for beginners in August 2025*. Bankrate.

Monefy Editorial Team. (2025, June 3). *Best Investment Platforms in 2025*. Monefy.

Benson, A. (2025, August 1). *Best Brokers for Beginner Investors: Top Picks for 2025*. NerdWallet.

SmartAsset. (2025, April). *5 Popular Investment Types and Strategies for Young Adults*. SmartAsset.

Baker, B. (2025, February 04). *How to invest in your 20s: 7 tips to get started*. Bankrate.

Fidelity Investments. (2024, June 03). *How to start investing as a teenager*. Fidelity.com.

Viva Koutour Cosmetics. (2025, January 15). *Profitable Side Hustles in 2025: Turn Your Passion into Profit*. Viva Koutour Cosmetics.

Ferguson, E. (2025, May 29). *30 Side Hustle Ideas That Don't Need Experience*. Shopify Blog.

Amber Student. (2024, January 22). *12 Best Online Side Hustles You Should Try In 2025*. Amber Student Blog.

Blake, T. (2025, January). *15 Best Digital Side Hustles To Start In 2025*. The Budget Diet.

Rainey, J. (2023, August 18). *Mastering Time Management: A Guide for Small Business Owners*. Jenna Rainey.

Accion Opportunity Fund. (2025, March 11). *Time Management for Business: Best Practices & Tools*. Accion Opportunity Fund.

Memon, S. (2024, August 13). *The Ultimate Guide to Time Management for Entrepreneurs: Strategies for Success*. ASU Entrepreneurship + Innovation.

Hall, J. (2024, October 18). *Time is Money: A Guide to Effective Time Management for Entrepreneurs*. Calendar.

Deloitte Center for Technology, Media & Telecommunications. (2025, March 25). *2025 Digital Media Trends: Social platforms are becoming a dominant force in media and entertainment*. Deloitte Insights.

Walsh, G. (2025, January 1). *Social media statistics for brands in 2025*. GWI.

Kelley, S. (2023, November). *Digital Marketing Trends in 2025: The Complete Guide*. TheeDigital.

Sprout Social. (2025, February). *Social media demographics to inform your 2025 strategy*. Sprout Social.

Badalyan, A. (2025, February 20). *55 Social Media Statistics For 2025: Trends, Insights & Marketing Impact*. Digital Silk.

Gimarino, J. (2024, November 11). *Building a Strong Financial Foundation: Tips for Young Adults*. The Lantern Network.

Truong, B. (2024, May 14). *10 Tips in Financial Planning to Give Young Adults a Head Start*. Wellby Financial.

Flatwater Bank. (2023, December 15). *A Young Adults Guide to Take Control of Finances*. Flatwater Bank.

United States Senate Federal Credit Union. (2023, December 1). *Senate Cents: A Financial Wellness Blog*. USSFCU.

Admin. (2025, February 24). *Mastering Self-Employment Taxes with Diverse Income Streams in 2025*. FileLater.

Internal Revenue Service. (2024, October 22). *IRS releases tax inflation adjustments for tax year 2025*. IRS.gov.

Jesseca Lane. (2025, January 29). *Managing Multiple Incomes for 2025 Side Hustle Taxes*. Palm Finance.

Magone & Co. (2025, January 03). *Active Income vs. Passive Income: Breaking Down the Tax Consequences*. Magone CPAs.

The Muse Editor. (2024, February 12). *16 Passive Income Ideas for Young Adults*. The Muse.

Almeda, A. J. (2025, January). *14 Passive Income Ideas for Young Adults*. UG Payments.

Perkins, G. (2023, May 9). *Passive Income Ideas That Are Actually Worth Your Time*. Gillian Perkins.

Weaver, R. & Siviter, A. (2024, October 22). *Top Real Estate Investment Strategies for Beginners*. Trout CPA.

Tirios. (2024, December 5). *Best way to start investing in real estate investing at a young age*. Tirios.ai.

Farther. (2024, January 1). *Essential Real Estate Investment Strategies In 2025*. Farther.

Lodha. (2024, June 03). *Building Wealth Early: A Guide to Real Estate Investing for Young Adults*. Lodha Group.

Kirk, V. (2023, September 26). *Real Estate Investing for Beginners: 5 Skills of Successful Investors*. Harvard Division of Continuing Education Professional Development.

J.P. Morgan Research. (2025, April 15). *US Housing Market Outlook*. J.P. Morgan.

RealtyHack. (2025, January). *Real Estate Market Trends: What to Expect in 2025*. RealtyHack.

Dehan, A. (2025, July 15). *Housing market predictions for the rest of 2025*. Bankrate.

PricewaterhouseCoopers. (2024, February 1). *Emerging Trends in Real Estate® 2025*. PwC.

Dollars and Sense Publishing. (2024, September 30). *Financial Literacy Essentials: A Dollars and Sense Guide to Budgeting, Saving, Investing and More for Teens and Young Adults*. Goodreads.

Saving Benjamins. (2025, May 10). *Foolproof Guide to Financial Literacy for Young Adults: Master Saving, Curb Overspending, Manage Student Debt and Achieve True Independence*. Amazon.

Money Mentor Publications. (2024, November 01). *The Complete Financial Literacy Collection 2 Books in 1: 2 Books in 1: A Fun & Easy Step-by-Step Guide for Kids, Teens & Young Adults to Master Smart Money Habits, Achieve Financial Security, and Grow Wealth with Ease*. Indigo.

McLaren, A. (2025, June 13). *Financial Literacy for Teens and Young Adults: Money Skills to Build Wealth & Still Have Fun*. Amazon.com.

Chicago Association of REALTORS. (2023, October 15). *Essentials of Property Management*. Chicago Association of REALTORS.

Fixflo. (2024, April 30). *The ultimate guide to property management in 2024*. Fixflo.

FirstService Residential. (2025, April 02). *What is Property Management?*. FirstService Residential Virginia.

UpKeep Media. (2017, November 01). *Property Management Tips: How to Be a Good Property Manager*. UpKeep Media.

KEW Legal. (2025, April). *Comprehensive Guide to Real Estate Risk Management: Strategies, Tools, and Compliance Tips for Safer Investments*. KEW Legal.

Merit Abode Nigeria Limited. (2024, January). *Effective Strategies for Managing Risk in Real Estate*. Merit Abode.

Embroker Team. (2024, August 5). *Real Estate Risk Management: Threats Facing the Industry*. Embroker.

Connect Invest. (2022, February 26). *Real Estate Investing at a Young Age*. Connect Invest.

Lainiotis, G. I. (2023, August 19). *Personal Finance for Teens and Young Adults: Financial Literacy Skills To Empower Your Future, Crush Your Debt & Build Smart Money Habits That Instill Lifelong Confidence*. Walmart.com.

www.ingramcontent.com/pod-product-compliance
Lightning Source LLC
Chambersburg PA
CBHW051413050726

47595CB00010B/4055